BRIGHT

CW00540126

THE STRANGER AND OTHER WORKS BY ALBERT CAMUS

Intelligent Education

IP **INFLUENCE PUBLISHERS**

Nashville, Tennessee

BRIGHT NOTES: The Stranger and Other Works

www.BrightNotes.com

No part of this publication may be used or reproduced in any manner whatsoever without written permission, except in the case of brief quotations in critical articles and reviews. For permissions, contact Influence Publishers http://www.influencepublishers.com.

ISBN: 978-1-645420-04-0 (Paperback)
ISBN: 978-1-645420-05-7 (eBook)

Published in accordance with the U.S. Copyright Office Orphan Works and Mass Digitization report of the register of copyrights, June 2015.

Originally published by Monarch Press.
Armand Schwerner; Laurie Rozakis; Austin Fowler, 1965
2020 Edition published by Influence Publishers.

Interior design by Lapiz Digital Services. Cover Design by Thinkpen Designs.

Printed in the United States of America.

Library of Congress Cataloging-in-Publication Data forthcoming.
Names: Intelligent Education
Title: BRIGHT NOTES: The Stranger and Other Works
Subject: STU004000 STUDY AIDS / Book Notes

CONTENTS

ALBERT CAMUS

INTRODUCTION

. . . .

PREFACE

The man who was to win the Nobel Prize for Literature in 1957 at the age of forty-four, was born on November 7, 1913, in the small village of Mondovi, Algeria. His father was a day laborer, a Frenchman of Alsatian descent. Called up for army service in 1914, for the First World War, he was killed, at thirty-four, in the battle of the Marne. Albert was one year old. His widowed mother, a Spaniard, illiterate, deaf, and given all her life to grave silences because of a speech impediment, moved to the Rue de Lyon in the Belcourt section of Algiers. Here in the working-class quarter-crowded, poor beyond imagination, but pulsing with life under the fecund Algerian sun-she supported her family as a cleaning woman. Albert and his older brother grew up under the domineering supervision of a grandmother, a harsh and unloving woman dying of cancer of the liver. With them in the two-room apartment there also lived a partially paralyzed uncle. These were the forces, the situations out of which Camus was shaped: the dead father, the dying grandmother, the paralyzed uncle, the deaf and silent mother, the poverty, and, opposed to these, the sun. Death surrounded his early years as it surrounded most of his life; but there was also the pure vitalism of the sun. With these opposites of existence he struggled all his life, seeking a reconciliation. Human existence was brief, painful, inevitably annihilated: this was "absurd." But beyond this absurdity there was a position which was not absurd, one which had meaning.

THE SILENT MOTHER

He sought, as he said himself, to give voice to the "silent mother," who symbolized the poor, the inarticulate, the disenfranchised who live at the bottom of the ladder of existence. For them he wished to speak.

The people of Belcourt were of many origins: French, Spanish, Italian, Maltese, Jewish. They filtered into the hard and sun dominated land of Algeria, with its terrible deserts, its rocky coasts washed by the blue Mediterranean, its fields and trees and towns and beaches baked under the lemon sun, and its very poverty forced them into a democracy of existence. For Camus they were all "his" people: European, Arabic, Berber. Their customs, evolved out of generations of sufferings endured, gave Camus his fundamental understanding of humanity. It was an understanding as Germaine Bree says in her biography of Camus (see Bibliography), "untouched by middle-class inhibitions and codes of conduct."

EARLY SCHOOLING

In such a world Camus spent the first twenty-seven years of his life. But genius and the "luck" which seems always to attend it were already leading Camus out of the existence which would have inevitably been his. In the grade school of Belcourt there happened to be an inspiring and discerning teacher named Louis Germain. When Camus entered school in 1918, Germain took interest in the boy, helped him in after-school projects, and prepared him to win the scholarship which would send him to the lycee (something like the American high school but started earlier) in Algiers. Camus entered the lycee in 1923, at the age of ten; the course of studies he followed there prepared him to enter the University of Algiers, where he studied philosophy from 1932 to 1936. Camus dedicated his Nobel Prize speech to Louis Germain.

THE SEA

In the lycee, although a superior student, Camus's primary interest was sports, especially soccer, in which he excelled as a goalkeeper. And he swam. Swimming was more than a sport to him. It was an activity of the body so important to him that the pages he devoted to the analysis of its joys are among the loveliest and most important he ever wrote. The sea was the opposite of the town; there, rolling in the water, browning in the sun, was free existence. The sea seems always to have the force for Camus of the great sea of Plotinus, the ancient African philosopher. Man came from the sea and must return to it. The sea is man's natural element: in it he finds freedom.

TUBERCULOSIS

But the free and exultant joy of the body was not to last. In 1930 Camus suffered a violent attack of tuberculosis. In the public wards of the hospital at Algiers, the encounter with death-his own death-was traumatic. It represented a turning point in his life. He left home and supported himself. His mind developed rapidly. He dedicated himself with feverish activity to reading, writing, and working. For the first time, he was made aware of the unique importance of life, of his life. He had seen death. Life became more precious. It was the only thing there was.

FIRST WRITINGS

At the University Camus' ambition was to be a teacher. Because of his illness, he would not, however, have been able to pass the medical examination required for the license. This and other, more obscure factors of talent and circumstance led him to dedicate himself fully to writing. During the next years, until 1938, when he earned his living as a journalist, he held many jobs: tutor, meteorologist, salesman, clerk. But he wrote all the time. In 1935 he began to keep notebooks (which have now been published: see Bibliography) in which he jotted plans, thoughts, observations. Under the influence of his master in philosophy at the University (Jean Genier) he began to write essays. Two volumes of these were eventually published in Algiers: "L'Envers et L'endroit" (1937) and "Noces" (1938). These will be discussed more fully later in this text. He wrote a novel (never published) which is, in many ways, a preparatory draft of *The Stranger*. He completed a philosophical thesis for his degree at the University. In 1934 he joined (as did many others) the Communist party. Curiously enough, it was his membership in the party which led him to the theater and play writing.

EARLY THEATER EXPERIENCE

In the thirties the Communists tended to cultivate a close working relationship between the working classes and intellectuals. They sponsored various activities of a cultural nature, among others theaters and theater workshops. In 1935, at the initiative of Camus, Le Theatre du Travail (Worker's Theater) was organized in Algiers. At first committed to Communist doctrine, it outlasted this commitment and survived until the catastrophic days of 1939. For this theater Camus wrote, directed, and acted. He also adapted plays and novels. During this time he developed his lifelong passion for the stage, which was to flower in such powerful works as *Caligula* and *The Possessed*. From the theater he was also to gain immeasurably in the ability to objectify his material, to create characters and give them authentic speaking voices. His ability to describe and analyze was already masterful. The combination of all these factors would help him to create the worlds of *The Stranger* and *The Plague*.

THE WAR

In 1939, Camus was twenty-six. He had published his two books of essays. He was gaining considerable fame in Algeria for his work in the theater. His tuberculosis was in abeyance. He was leading a life full of productive activity. He was full of plans. He wanted to go to Greece, a country whose traditions and landscape had long attracted him. But then the Second World War broke over Europe, and nothing was to be the same again. The values which Camus had evolved for himself, a positive and pagan ethic of acceptance in a world otherwise nihilistic, were to be tested. In a sense, the large and continuous production of novels, articles, essays, short stories, plays, lectures, and letters which poured from Camus' pen from 1939 until the end of his life are attempts to show how these values may be applied in an "absurd" existence. The ancient and traditional structures of meaning which European culture had developed were, seemingly, destroyed overnight. For millions, existence became meaningless, absurd. In this atmosphere of cataclysmic anarchy and nihilism, the values of existence which Camus had developed for himself suddenly took on a universal validity. The terrible times were to find a voice, and in the voice meaning.

THE NONCOMBATANT COMBATANT

The war for Camus was stupid. But his father had died for France. He tried to enlist but, because of his health, was refused. He left Algiers and, having worked first in the Algerian city of Oran (setting of *The Plague*), he went to Paris, where he worked as a journalist on the *Paris-Soir*. There in May of 1940, he finished *The Stranger*, just before the German invasion. He moved to the manufacturing city of Lyons, and there finished "The Myth of Sisyphus." In January of 1941 he returned to Algeria. For the next three years he read, worked, meditated, planned, and continued his involvement in the theater. He produced *Hamlet* in 1941. It was not until the execution of a prominent anti-Nazi in France that Camus actively committed himself to fighting the German conquerors.

COMBAT

In 1943 he joined the underground group called "Combat." For it he edited a news sheet also called Combat. The hundreds of articles which Camus wrote for this paper form a record of the reactions of a highly trained, sensitive, intelligent man of genius to the monstrosities of war. In the dark night of Europe, it was, for thousands of Frenchmen, a source of information, of stimulation, of comfort. Most of all it was a demonstration of the survival of tradition, of a judicial intelligence, of a moral standard, when all these seemed otherwise to have been washed away in the floods of hatred and debauchery. The anonymous editor continued his task unremittingly; his name did not come to light until August 21, 1944, the first day of the battle for the liberation of Paris, when the name Albert Camus, no longer required to be hidden, was blazoned forth as director. But by then the name of Camus was already famous, as the author of the amazing novel *The Stranger* and the incredible essay "The Myth of Sisyphus."

EARLY SUCCESS

The publication of *The Stranger* (*L'Etranger*) in 1942 and "The Myth of Sisyphus" ("Le Mythe de Sisyphe") in 1943 had brought Camus instantaneous success. His hard, elegant, lucid, and sensuous prose was in the great classic tradition of French literature: he was immediately recognized as a master. But this in itself would not have been sufficient cause for the acclaim with which these works were greeted. The subject of the works, the philosophic assumptions on which they were grounded, the ideas which they ruthlessly analyzed were propitious for the times. In them, as Philip Thody (see Bibliography) says, there is "a philosophical view of the universe in which . . . all optimism [was] suppressed . . ."; this "corresponded exactly to the historical situation of the French people." Meursault, the central character of *The Stranger*, is characterized by a total indifference to everything in existence except the physical sensations of the moment. These physical sensations constitute for him the only experiences that are valid and trustworthy. Aside from these the world is absurd and meaningless. Everyone about him demands that he have emotions which he cannot feel; he refuses to feel them. To "act" as if he felt them for the conveniences of convention would, for him, be false and unauthentic. He refuses to "act." This refusal leads to his condemnation and death. This demand for the authentic, this insistence on uncompromising fidelity to what is made valid by one's own experience is what is new in literature. It is what appealed to the Europe of the occupation. "The Myth of Sisyphus," written just after *The Stranger*, is a statement of Meursault's philosophy. Together the two books form the objective human experience and the philosophical analysis of it. One makes the other understandable.

LETTERS TO A GERMAN FRIEND

During these next year's Camus continued to write. He worked on *The Plague* and "The Rebel." During the Resistance, however, among his hundreds of articles, he wrote four cast in the form of letters. These were published in 1945 as *Letters to a German Friend*. In them he outlined his personal creed. He establishes that his ethic is not the development of a logical position but the outcome of personal experience. "His logic," says Bree, "is the logic of life and death, not the logic of philosophy."

THE CULTURE HERO

When it became known that the anonymous director of Combat was the author of *The Stranger* and "The Myth of Sisyphus," Camus' fame increased immeasurably. He became, almost overnight, the voice of conscience in both politics and ethics. Jean-Paul Sartre, of whom more later, hailed him: "You had all the luck and all the merits, bringing to a sense of greatness a passionate love of beauty, to the joy of living, the sense of death . . . How we loved you then." In 1944 Camus was thirty-one. Independently, courageously, following no party line, continuing to make judgments only on the basis of his personal experiences, he wrote during the next years, and up until his death, on every subject that demanded a position. He had rejected Marxism. Now he became the target of Communist attack. He formed a political party to provide a non-Marxist rallying point for working people. It failed. His activities continued to be prodigious. At an age when most men have either not earned substantial fame or are just entering upon it, Camus had a reputation almost unmatched in the postwar era. The demands on his time were continuous and exhausting. Nevertheless he continued to create at an amazing rate.

OTHER WORKS

Besides his work for the publisher Gallimard as a reader and editor, his two lecture tours which brought him to the United States in 1946-47 and to South America in 1949, he wrote and published in rapid succession four plays: *The Misunderstanding* in 1944, *Caligula* in 1945, *The State of Siege* in 1948, and *The Just Assassins* in 1949. In 1947 he published the second of his novels, *The Plague*, and in 1951 the second of his book-length essays, "The Rebel." From 1949 to 1951 he suffered a new attack of tuberculosis. The result of this attack was similar to the result of the attack at seventeen. That first attack had changed the course of his life: before it he had been satisfied with the joys of pure physical existence; after it he pursued with the same fury and intensity the development of his mind. After the attack of 1949-51, he withdrew from politics into silence, nourishing and developing his spirit. Until 1956 he published no more major work. Then he published his adaptation as a play of Faulkner's novel *Requiem for a Nun*; he also directed this play in Paris. The theater was to assume more and more importance in his life; again, after twenty years, he had come back to it.

THE NOBEL PRIZE

In the fifties, Camus published continuously; there were many adaptations of plays and novels, including *Requiem for a Nun*, already mentioned, and *The Possessed*, from Dostoevsky's novel of the same name. In 1956 he published *The Fall*, his last novel. In 1957 *Exile and the Kingdom*, a collection of short stories, was published. His fame increased. In 1957, he was awarded the Nobel Prize for Literature. At forty-four, he was, perhaps, the youngest person ever to be given this honor. He had entered the company of those few whom the world acknowledges as its greatest writers.

LAST DAYS

He felt himself full of works to come. He worked on a new novel, to be called *The First Man*, and a play, to be called *Don Juan*. In 1959, Andre Malraux, President De Gaulle's minister of culture, and himself a writer of the greatest reputation, offered Camus the directorship of a theater; it was enthusiastically accepted. Then on January 4, 1960, at the age of forty-five, the Nobel Prize winner, novelist, philosopher, playwright, moralist, short-story writer, theater director, Resistance leader, and tubercular adolescent from the slums of Algiers was killed, abruptly, when the car in which he was riding as a passenger struck a tree. In his pocket was the railway ticket which he had chosen not to use. Many were struck by the "absurdity" of this loss. He was laid in state in the small town hall of Villeblevin; later his remains were transported to the village of Lourmarin in the south of France where he had been living. There, in the small cemetery of the village he was buried, far from "the black sun" of Algeria.

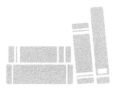

ALBERT CAMUS

. . . .

THE MYTH OF SISYPHUS, THE REBEL, AND OTHER ESSAYS

The notion that life is "rational" comes primarily from the Greeks. As early as Homer, we may note the large areas of reality which have come under the domination of intelligence, and the growing assumption culminating in the encyclopedic work of Aristotle that existence can be made understandable to reason. Generally speaking, at the back of this assumption there are two other assumptions at work: that mind is separately and distinct from matter, and that reality (as "an object," or continuum of discrete, separate, interconnected "objects") can be classified, or mapped. The inevitable result of this approach is a dichotomy, or double mode of existence. Man (as "mind") though an "object" in reality, is at the same time somehow apart from it. Existence then becomes known by its systematization into a gridwork of rules: rules of logic, rules of conduct, rules of behavior. Every subject (object) can be understood insofar as it is objectified and systematized. For the thousands of years from the Greeks to the present, this basic relationship between the individual and the rest of existence has consciously or unconsciously been held valid in the Western world. Until the twentieth century most men, with certain notable exceptions, believed that the "map" which tradition had made available to them was a true, valid explanation of reality.

THE "ABSURD"

However, for many men of the twentieth century, Camus among them, this old map ceased to be valid. It no longer made sense. Life could no longer be understood by means of it. Existence, far from being the orderly and illuminated thing tradition said it was, was, in fact, chaotic, meaningless, "absurd." The rejection of the tradition was thoroughgoing. Men became nihilistic; they accepted nothing (nihil) as valid, given, true. Some chose merely to denounce, violently, bitterly. They felt betrayed and were furious because of the betrayal. Some, freed from the restraints of the old logic, saw existence as merely a joke and made a philosophy of their conclusion (the Dadaists, for instance). Other retreated from life to one extent or another, even to that total retreat of suicide. Camus, having recognized the situation, explored it more profoundly. "The Myth of Sisyphus" is the result of his analysis of the situation and his attempt to make sense of it. We cannot understand his novels or plays without understanding his essays.

THE MYTH OF SISYPHUS

Camus began to work on the essay as early as 1938. During those years he had already come to the conclusion that he was a nihilist, that the traditional explanations were insufficient. And yet there was in him a strong reaction against the despair and pessimism which seemed the only "logical" stance to take as the result of his discovery of the "absurd." He wanted to be happy. He regarded happiness as a categorical imperative of human existence. This question then is the central question with which "The Myth of Sisyphus" deals: given the meaninglessness of existence, how can a man be happy? The book then is a more or less systematic investigation of the position of "l'homme absurde" (man as absurd). The work as published breaks into not so much one single production as a series or set of essays concerned with the same subject.

Camus was quite a young man when he wrote the essay. Perhaps it is for this reason that the notion of happiness is his primary concern. But, in spite of his youth, he realized the need for the total eradication of the illusions which prevent one from seeing the condition of absurdity. So the first section of "The Myth of Sisyphus" is concerned with a ruthless dissection of the human condition as Camus sees it. He does this in order to lay bare the sickness which is at the root of contemporary sensibility. Man is sick, but he does not know the cause of his sickness. Like a physician, Camus set out to diagnose the disease, and then offer a cure. His purpose is ethical and positive. He demanded happiness; he said that man could be and should be happy. But he would never be happy until he understood what was making him unhappy. The young men, especially those of intelligence, of the twenties and thirties were the heirs of the terrible malady of spirit of the 1880-1890's, the so-called fin de siecle. Skeptical, pessimistic, world weary, their spirits corroded by nihilism, they concluded that life was a farce, a sort of joke. How could one seriously participate in a joke? What Camus insisted on was that accepting nihilism as an end was defeatist, self-pitying, and a type of Romanticism. He addresses his essay particularly to this audience of pessimists, evolving before them the logic necessity in such a situation, that suicide is the only out, but, having reached this extreme, he rejects it as the wrong answer. The limit of human existence having been noted, it is for man to revolt against this limit, accept life within the boundaries of death and suffering, and in this acceptance find happiness.

Because life is incomprehensible, he says, it does not follow that it is meaningless. Such logic is false; it is based on the despair that follows from finding the traditional explanations of life (Greek-Judeo-Christian) false or inadequate. It is an emotional, not a reasonable conclusion. Certainly, life is absurd; it is also precious. Because it eludes us, because it cannot be reduced to human meaning-this is what makes it wonderful. Our human awareness is made more acute by the full understanding of our position in time. He denies the validity of the existential approach. Contrary to popular opinion Camus was not an existentialist; indeed, he not only denied he was one of them, he even refuted their assumptions and conclusions. He says that the existentialists give arbitrary meaning to what is in fact meaningless. They are, in effect, rationalists turned inside out. No, he says, one must accept with total awareness and complete consciousness, the fact that life has no meaning that is beyond itself. All the approaches which demand of existence something beyond the moment, transcendent of life, beyond life, at the end of "history," outside of time or beyond time or at the end of time are the result of man's refusal to face facts. There is man, there is nature. That is all. Man finds whatever meaning he is to find by acknowledging that fact.

Comment

Camus denied categorically that he was a philosopher. He has a philosophy, but by his denial he meant to emphasize that his answers to the problems of existence are those which, haphazardly, circumstantially, arose out of his own confrontation with life and insisted on being answered. Unlike Jean-Paul Sartre, in whose company he is often placed, he made no attempt at a systematic, point-by-point elucidation of a complete metaphysic. Out of his own temperament, with the specific tools of mind and sensibility he had to hand, he faced certain obstacles and, because of his honesty and integrity, sought their cause and effect. The validity of his analysis and the power of his solutions are the validity and power which result from the personal courage to see clearly and react clearly. He is one who does not falsify data. His approach to the problem of suicide and the problem of happiness follows the tempo and curve of his personal fate. Everything he says is said out of experience, the concrete, the tangible. All he knew was that in spite of the terrible poverty of his youth, in spite of the deprivation and pain and sufferings of that time, he had been happy. In a sense, all his work is an attempt to create an order in the world which would make that primal happiness of the body and the sun available to him again and to all men. Any approach to man's existence which puts the possible happiness of the present after a happiness in the future (which may or may not come) is to be denied. In this initial position we find Camus' strength; it is why he denied Christianity, "historicity," much philosophy, and totalitarianism in all its forms, including the totalitarianism of the Right (fascism) and of the Left (communism). They all put the system's success before the individual's happiness.

THE ONE PHILOSOPHICAL PROBLEM

Camus opens his essay by announcing that "There is only one really serious philosophical problem." This problem is suicide. However, there are suicides and suicides. He is concerned here not with those which occur because of terror, or unbearable mental or physical pain, or out of pique or insanity. He focuses on those suicides which are precisely the result of holding that life is meaningless and therefore not worth living. The precise question then is laid bare: is suicide a solution to the realization that life is absurd?

In the next section, he defines the meaning of "the absurd." People, pacified by the pap of routine, go about their business; they get up, they eat, they dress, go to work, eat, digest, play, sleep. This is unending. Or apparently. One day, out of nowhere, the question strikes one, "Why?" Tradition and the dedicated philosophers and maintainers of tradition quiet us. They have answers. "Wait," "You'll understand," "The future will disclose all." But in the meanwhile one's life disappears. We revolt. But this revolt in itself is an aspect of absurdity.

Then too there is the sense of dislocation from the objects about us, the strange disquietude which sets in when, briefly, we note the inhumanity of humanity, the divorce between our assumptions about what men should be and our sudden recognition of what they are. This extends even to ourselves when unexpectedly our self-awareness, like a bird, flies to a distance, and watching, does not recognize what it sees: "the familiar yet disquieting brother we recognize in our own photographs. . . ." This dislocation and divorce is also "absurd."

And there is the final aspect of the recognition of the absurd: Death. This is not the knowledge that men die, that nature is a death in life, a life in death, that loved ones die, that enemies die. The resounding crash of awareness which comes when one sees and understands that he will die brings the final realization of the absurd. This "bloody mathematics which orders our existence" can be given no real and acceptable acceptance by any code or system of knowledge.

Such an understanding of one's condition produces, as Sartre says, "nausea," anxiety and tension and disgust. But there are ways which men have evolved for dealing with this situation. Let us set them out and see how well they work. All of them, he finds, are based on the substitution of terms, on nostalgia, on wishful thinking, on emotion rather than reason. Reason itself can do nothing to introduce motives of hope. Religion is equally incapable. No, one is not facing the fact. One can touch the world, see it, taste it, touch it, smell it: that is all one can affirm; the rest is fancy. "I shall always be an outsider to myself - and to the world." We do not live forever. We must therefore live and live fully the life that we have.

Camus systematically and rather curtly cuts off all the exits of hope. Man, each one of us, dies. Unlike all else in creation, we know we die. Indeed, there is nothing else of any depth we know about our condition. Is therefore suicide, as it appears to be, the logical answer? No, to take one's life is precisely to deny the one existence we have. It makes death important when it is merely a limit, a terminal point. Suicide is, in the credo of life, an act of faithlessness. Man must, finally, accept his condition with total lucidity. It is just because life has no extension beyond the limits of birth and death that one must embrace it with passion. One must "revolt" against death, and anything which makes death meaningful.

Comment

In his early books of essays (*Betwixt and Between* and *Nuptials*) Camus had already recognized the absurdity of life as he experienced it. His confrontation with death in the hospital wards of Algiers had served to shock him awake. Up to this time, he had lived the thoughtless life of the body in the sun. His existence then had an almost primitive quality about it. He and the physical world were one. In *Nuptials* his subject is the union, the marriage, of the life-giving sun with nature of which he himself was a part. His personal experience had demonstrated the falsity of all modes of hope for life beyond death. None of the available systems had answered his persistent questions: why death, what is the meaning of life? He revolted, then, against the placid acceptance of death and sought to attain a union with existence as it is. "The Myth of Sisyphus" is an analysis of the situation in which he then found himself, and record of how he escaped it.

"L'HOMME ABSURDE"

Having demonstrated to the reader the condition of man as, in his belief, he is, and with ruthless logic shown that there is no hope to be found in the religious or philosophic systems which man has evolved to face the absurd, Camus then goes on to characterize the man who has accepted life as absurd without illusion. He calls him L'homme absurde. He lives without nostalgia. That he is in a prison he knows; he accepts the limits as there. But the very acceptance fills him with confident life. His one enemy is death. He revolts against death, against the "natural" order in which "death" has a meaning. Man revolts as part of his very humanity. To accept death is to diminish one's humanity. His hope is for life, not for the future or for the past. Life is replete with possibilities. These he accepts. These form his joy.

Comment

Later in life, when Camus was questioned about the "pessimism" in his work he was rather taken aback. He believed that there

THE STRANGER AND OTHER WORKS

was affirmation and optimism there. He said then that although he might be pessimistic about humanity, he was full of optimism about man. Humanity is an abstraction. Men are concrete.

A GALLERY OF MEN AS ABSURD

Camus' ethic concentrates on the particular and concrete. In the next section of "The Myth of Sisyphus" he creates a group of portraits of men, "or heroes," who may serve as models of those who accept life as absurd but live it passionately and with full awareness of its limits. Their code of honor, their commitment is as deep and full as that of the medieval knights, the Japanese samurai, the missionaries of any religion or philosophy. They put their lives totally on the line, they are fully engaged. They are "great men." They are the opposite of frivolous.

The first of these is Don Juan. For him the passionate diversity of existence was expressed in the specific and concrete relationship he had with each of his multitudes of women. Love was for him not mere liberty or license or hatred of sex or a method of despising women. It was an occasion for life; each encounter was a renewal of total engagement with existence. Never could he be, never did he wish to be, satisfied. For to be satisfied is to accept death. Don Juan's insatiable appetite for love was an insatiable appetite for life. It constituted a lifelong revolt, not against religion, or the establishment, or custom as such, but against death.

The next hero, or model of L'homme absurde is the actor. (Camus was, as the reader knows, deeply involved in the theater as playwright, director, actor. He said on one occasion that he was never so happy as when he was on the stage. Among other roles he played Hamlet in his own production in Algiers in the

1940's. Of all Shakespeare's characters, many of whom are actors, Hamlet is perhaps the most diverse.) Why is the actor an example of l'homme absurde? Because, taking on many roles, he lives each with tremendous and passionate intensity upon the stage. He pours out his substance into the shell of the character he knows exists only the hour or two he incarnates him. Here is, in little, a perfect example of the full, vital life within absolutely known limits. The death of the character when the curtain goes down, the many, many deaths of Hamlet which the actor experiences, do not affect him any more than his own death. The character ceases. He has lived; he ceases. So man. He lives, he ceases. This does not mean the character on the stage should be any less lively or passionate because the actor playing him knows he will die. On the contrary the realization of death to come fills the actor with the desire to make each second of stage life more complete. It has always been the case that man sees the stage life of characters as larger than life. This merely demonstrates that most men are not living life to the full.

The next model is that of the "conqueror." This conqueror, however, is not the familiar figure of school history who subjugates peoples and territories. No he is quite the opposite. He is the man who knows that "history" is an error, that those who act in the name of history to carry out plans for "humanity" are wrong. He fights this knowing that he will probably lose; he contradicts with his "absurd" conscience the forces which forever try to use man for purposes beyond life.

Comment

When Camus denounced totalitarianisms of every variety, when he carried on his argument with Sartre, he was acting precisely as this "conqueror." When Camus published his second philosophical essay, "The Rebel," Sartre, with whom Camus had for many years been allied, broke with him precisely over this point. Sartre had, although not a Communist, supported the Communist position, even apparently, the need to destroy and imprison human beings "for the cause." Camus refused to condone or justify this even if it were demonstrated that the humanity "of the future" was aided by these acts.

SISYPHUS

The next and last example of l'homme absurde is the greatest of them all. He is Sisyphus, the hero of the Greek myth. Sisyphus had been condemned by the gods to roll a great stone everlastingly to the top of a mountain. There at the top and of its own weight it would roll down to the valley again and the task would begin again. This hopeless and totally useless task was, in the opinion of the gods, the worse form of punishment they could inflict on a man. Why had the gods inflicted this punishment? Because Sisyphus, having died, and having been allowed by Pluto (god of the underworld) to return briefly to the world, failed to honor his word and return to the land of the dead. Sisyphus is the great hero because of his disdain for the gods, his hatred of death, his love of life. His punishment, although useless, is not meaningless. The greatest glory of man is expending all his substance and existence to achieve precisely nothing.

Comment

Sisyphus is of course a symbol of man. The rock is man's awareness of the absurdity of his existence. Camus' position is that Sisyphus is fully alive and as such expresses his potential fully. He cannot waste any vitality in dreaming or in false hope;

he is forced by his knowledge to extract joy from the given, for he knows that there is nothing else. Sisyphus, in the monotonous limits of his task, is an extreme case. It is just because he is an extreme case that he is a good example. It is also worth noting that at the basis of the story of Sisyphus there is a solar myth; that is, an attempt to explain the "eternal" movement of the sun, which seems to be rolled up to the height of the heavens and then rolls down the other side. This eternally recurrent task seems purposeless, but without the sun there would be no light, no life. It is curious to note that in Camus the sun holds the same central importance as it does for Wallace Stevens, the American poet, whose fundamental philosophy was almost identical with Camus. Stevens has a poem called "The Hero," which is simply about the rising and setting of the sun. Sisyphus, struggling towards the top of the mountain, knows that he will never reach it; he continues to try. That is his greatness. That is man's greatness.

CONCLUSIONS

Man must, says Camus, first face nihilism: there is no answer to death. But suicide is cowardice. Man has only one reality-life. He must live it. He can only live it by accepting its limits. That it has no meaning beyond itself is not a cause for pessimism. On the contrary it is the very foundation of our revolt against death, the fundamental reason why we should live it fully. One has then the duty to be happy. This notion of duty becomes the radical tenet of Camus' ethic. One should not only engage fully in existence for one's happiness; it is necessary, like "the conqueror," to engage, with all one's strength, for the happiness of others. We recognize that we are brothers, with the one commitment, because we are all to face death. Don Juan is praiseworthy because of his desire for life, but Sisyphus is the great hero because he symbolizes the more profound duty to push upward, to expand the limits of existence, while recognizing that the limits are there.

Comment

All Camus' heroes are outsized and extreme. His book, however, is directed to the ordinary man. How then can the ordinary man live the life of l'homme absurde? The essay, except insofar as one learns from the analysis of the examples offered, teaches little. It is in the extended portrait of Meursault, the "hero" of *The Stranger*, that this omission is rectified.

ESSAY QUESTIONS AND ANSWERS

Question: What was Camus' purpose in writing "The Myth of Sisyphus?"

Answer: His purpose is, simply, to offer his readers a "way" of life. In this sense, Camus' purpose is similar to the purpose of the great ethical and religious leaders of the past, rather than to the purpose of a philosopher. What Camus does it not so much build a philosophy (as do Kant, Hegel, and Aristotle, for example) as offer a "philosophy of life." Underlying the passionate drive of the book is not so much the desire to teach as the desire to help. Many in the world to which he addressed the work were "sick", confused, dying of nihilism. He (and they) had found the traditional positions helpless to alleviate their condition. But he had found an answer. This answer he offers them for their relief. It is a "way" of life he offers, as do the ethical teachers of the past. For this reason, later on, he was often called a "lay saint."

Question: What precisely is Camus' "philosophy" in "The Myth of Sisyphus?"

Answer: To summarize, Camus says that there is nothing that man really knows except that he dies. Realizing this, man has clutched at all sorts of ways out of this knowledge. He accepts the various straws of hope which various people have offered: that there is a life after death, that there is a meaning to history, and so on. But no one knows that these ideologies are correct. What one does know is that there is death. Having accepted this nihilism what should one do? Some commit suicide. But this is ridiculous, cowardly, and a misunderstanding of the position. That life is incomprehensible does not make it meaningless. One must accept with total lucidity that death is there, but only to deny it, reject it, revolt against it. Life can only be lived to the fullest when it is accepted for what it is in itself. There is joy, there is happiness, there is everything.

Question: How does Camus' use of the term "absurd" differ from Jean-Paul Sartre's?

Answer: Sartre defines the absurd as a realization of man's transiency, his division from the continuum of existence, his belief that in the universe there is no real place for him. Hence his "nausea," his terror, his sense of divorce and accidental presence. Sartre defines the term as a philosopher. Camus uses it as an ethical notion. For Camus the absurd was simply a part of human existence, to be accepted, as the Greeks did suffering and pain as part of the human lot, without attempting to explain it. But Camus says that, recognizing the absurd, one may then deny it by living passionately. The result of this is that the absurd disappears. The denial is a revolt which succeeds.

ALBERT CAMUS

THE STRANGER

....

INTRODUCTION

Up to the time of the publication of *The Stranger*, in 1942, whatever fame Camus enjoyed rested on the books of essays he had published in Algeria (*Betwixt and Between* and *Nuptials*). This is almost to say that he had no fame to speak of at all. Almost immediate renown came to him with *The Stranger*. It was more than anything else a question of the conjunction of the right time and the right book for that time. In 1942 the war had engulfed Europe. The old world and its order had been struck down in the general destruction. The traditional principles of behavior and the traditional system of rules by which men conducted, or believed they ought to conduct, their lives were suddenly meaningless. In the character of Meursault, Camus created an archetype for his time. For Meursault believes in nothing but the present, and the present known only through immediate physical sensations. He has not arrived at his point by argument, or by analysis. He is not a philosopher, nor is he merely a cynic. His temperament and sensibilities are such that he can only relate to the world in a certain way. His integrity and absolute honesty make it impossible for him to falsify his actions or his beliefs. He refuses to play a role tradition expects of him. He refuses to participate or conform for the sake of peace. He makes no demand except to live. But his refusal to conform leads to his death. In him Europeans discerned the very man so many of them had become. In his death and the illumination of the use of life he receives just before death they recognized a brother and a meaning. The "Stranger" was, in effect, not a stranger at all. In him they recognized themselves as in a mirror.

ANALYSIS AND COMMENTARY

"The Stranger," says Sartre in "An Explication of *The Stranger*," "[Camus] wants to portray is precisely one of those terrible innocents who shock society by not accepting the rules of its game," and "'The Myth of Sisyphus' teaches us how to accept our author's novel." If "The Myth of Sisyphus" gives us the idea of the absurd, *The Stranger* gives us the feeling. Meursault has his density as a character in a real world; he is not a thesis character, or a cut-out figure to which is attached a card identifying him as l'homme absurde. He is prior to any philosophy which explains him.

Meursault, writing in the first person, tells his own story. The form of the book is taken from Andre Gide, the journal and notebook of a man attempting to illuminate his past. But Meursault does not attempt to illuminate. He simply narrates and describes. What we learn about him is not the result of the passion for confession; it is a record. The meaning we find in the novel is the meaning we give it, not Meursault. His sentences are very much like Hemingway's; it is the short, staccato prose of the sensibility which distrusts abstraction. It is the recording style suited to a man in a face-to-face relationship with the continuum. It is always today of which he writes.

26

ESSAY QUESTIONS AND ANSWERS

Question: What is the relationship between the prose style of *The Stranger* and its meaning?

Answer: The prose of *The Stranger* is made up of short, explicit, clearly focused sentences. There is little cause-and-effect relationship between one statement and another. One thing is stated after another. The nouns are more important than the verbs. The tense is the present perfect. All these devices clearly mirror, support, and embody Meursault's fragmented, purely physical existence in which one sensation follows another. The meaning of the book is the experience the reader gets of such a world by being immersed in it. Sartre in his essay on the book says that in it one moves from sentence to sentence of clarity, but between the sentences there is chaos, the blank of absurdity. Camus has chosen, or invented, the perfect prose to convey his meaning.

Question: What are some of the major symbols of *The Stranger*?

Answer: Three elements take on great significance in *The Stranger*: the sea, the sun, the prison. We will take them in reverse order. The prison symbolizes, insofar as Meursault is typical, the cage in which man exists. A number of times in the novel, the note is sounded (notably by the chaplain) that all men are under sentence of death. It is what Meursault does with prison that is of the greatest significance: he accepts it. One day of life is sufficient to supply material to negate a hundred years of boredom. Others, being imprisoned, fall into ennui and suicidal boredom. Thus they live in the prison of existence. A second major symbol is the sea. For Meursault the sea signifies freedom and the source of life. What he misses most is not being able to swim in it. He recalls the sea and his swimming in it as giving him the moments of greatest joy. In it he could immerse himself totally and be one with the primal mother, carried by the fundamental rhythms of existence. The third is the sun, which is a more complex symbol. Meursault loves the sun; its presence floods the novel. But the sun is also lethal. At the moment of his crime the great cymbals of the sun beat in his head. In more than one way, the sun is responsible for the crime. It is difficult to say precisely what this double significance has in the novel except to say that the sun does give life and destroy it. It is worth nothing that as an Algerian, Camus was particularly aware of the destructive aspects of the sun, and as a Mediterranean he realized the need for moderation in its use. When Meursault kills the Arab, the beach had become a furnace of destruction.

Question: The character of Meursault has often been compared to the character of Julien Sorel in Stendhal's *The Red and The Black*. What is the worth of such a comparison?

Answer: The comparison is worthwhile more to show the differences between the two than to show their similarities. And the differences emphasizes the difference between the early ninteenth century, the Age of Napoleon, and the 1940's, the "Age of Hitler," Both Julien and Meursault are nonconformists, both kill a man, and both go to their deaths. There the similarities end. Julien's whole life is a demonstration of his will; he chooses his own destiny, he takes full responsibility for his acts. His hero is Napoleon. If one wishes, he is a symbol of Stendhal's belief in the demonic energy of the human will. At the end of his life, he chooses death. He would not return to the same life again. He has mastered it. Meursault, on the contrary, is a victim. He does not choose; he refuses to choose. Destiny is thrust upon him by a series of "chances" and "accidents." He does not control; he does not wish to control. At the end of his life he would gladly wish to live it over again, like Sisyphus, to go back and start the task over. His idea of afterlife is to remember this one. He does his job, but without ambition. In him there is no will, only sensation; no hope, only acceptance; no desire, only enjoyment.

Question: In every novel there is a conflict. What is the conflict in *The Stranger*?

Answer: The conflict in *The Stranger* is the contradiction which exists between the way in which Meursault experiences life and the way in which society expects him to experience it. This is made plainer to the reader, who has experienced the event with Meursault, when he hears the interpretation put upon Meursault's character and action by the lawyers at the trial. Because we know Meursault from one point of view (the existential), we react with dismay and exasperation to the Meursault which is the construction of abstractions (society's point of view). This double focus on the "real" Meursault produces tension. Meursault himself makes this distinction between seeing people and the world as abstractions (scientifically) and as loved objects (existentially) when he notes that the Persecutor keeps calling Marie "his mistress." "To me she was only Marie," he says. This conflict is essential to the meaning of the novel. To know the world scientifically, by abstractions, is only to know it at a distance. That is tantamount to not knowing it at all. There is only one way to know the world - through love. Looking at people scientifically leads to their "use." There is a scientific logic behind Hitler's gas ovens and the Stalinist labor camps. There is only one way to relate to the world and to the people in it - through love - unless one wishes to distort reality.

Question: What relationship is there between *The Stranger* and "The Myth of Sisyphus?"

29

Answer: *The Stranger* is the experience of Meursault, and "The Myth of Sisyphus" is the philosophy which grows out of and explains the significance of that experience. Or to put it a different way, *The Stranger* is the concrete, "The Myth of Sisyphus" is the abstract. They go together. It is as if, after writing *Hamlet*, Shakespeare had gone on to write a philosophical treatise embodying the philosophy upon which Hamlet acted, out of which his thoughts, emotions, reactions, and sensibility grew. To understand *The Stranger*, we need to read "The Myth of Sisyphus"; to get the full significance of "The Myth of Sisyphus" we need first to have experienced the existence of Meursault.

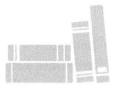

ALBERT CAMUS

THE PLAGUE

INTRODUCTION

Camus' second novel, *The Plague*, was published in 1947. Searching for a situation which would, within usable artistic limits, serve as a symbol of modern war, he hit upon the notion of a city visited by plague. This invention served him well on a number of levels and for a number of reasons. First of all the idea of war as a disease was congenial to him. It was especially congenial because the immediate context out of which he wrote was the Second World War, when the plague of Hitlerism had visited France. So France, like Oran, the city of the plague, was cut off from the outside world, quarantined by its infection. So in France, as in Oran, men reacted to the terrible visitation in different ways, according to their beliefs and characters. So in France, as in Oran, mutual disaster brought men together, and values were put to the supreme test; that is, what good are they tested against death. A plague is excess; excess is a disease. At the root of Nazism was an ideology of "all or nothing," the excess of ideology. And the plague is specifically the bubonic plague, the terrible plague which had afflicted Europe during medieval times and killed more than half its population. Significantly it was from Europe that the ideologies which have caused so many millions of deaths in the twentieth century have sprung. It is, therefore, easy to see in the plague of Oran the plague afflicting the modern world. But Camus does not, obviously, wish only to make a local identification. He is really concerned to show the plague as any form of pain, disaster, suffering, and terror which afflict mankind and how they can be resisted. The rebel here is not solitary. He finds, as he moves forward in his rebellion, that he shares with others a common task. This is what unites him to them. All men are oppressed.

THE MEANING OF THE PLAGUE

The Plague is cast in the form of an allegory. In an allegory the events, settings, and characters stand for something else besides themselves. In English, Bunyan's *Pilgrim's Progress* is perhaps the best-known allegory. In it Christian, the main character, is shown on his journey to the Celestial City, his proper home. On the way there he meets such characters as Despair and Hope; he must negotiate a swamp called "The Slough of Despond." Such an allegory is best called a "one-for-one" allegory - that is, there is a clear and limited identification of the elements with other elements for which they stand. A successful allegory is usually one in which the narrative is interesting for its own sake as well as for its message. The difficulties which the allegorist must overcome are two: he must make sure that the story hangs together and be interesting on its own; and he must make sure that the story maintains the desired relationship to the thing allegorized. It is extremely difficult, for instance, to understand all of the meaning of The Faerie Queene of Spenser because we have lost some of the keys to what he meant certain characters and events to stand for. That Camus wishes us to understand

The Plague as an allegory is clearly indicated by the epigraph from Daniel Defoe that stands at the front of the novel: "It is as reasonable to represent one kind of imprisonment by another, as it is to represent anything that really exists by that which exists not." What then does *The Plague* represent?

When the novel was first published the readers understood it to be an allegory of the state of Europe at the time. Oran, peaceful and unprepared, is overcome by the plague. France, peaceful and unprepared, is overcome by Nazism. France is segregated from the rest of the world, as is Oran. The average citizen is helpless to meet the plague in each situation. Certain men, however, do fight, each according to his means and capacities, in both situations. But does Camus' plague merely symbolize this single situation in history or does it have a wider application? No reader of the book, knowing Camus' general philosophy, can conclude that it has not a more universal meaning.

This meaning is insisted upon by the presence of Tarrou in the book. It is he who unites this particular and specific plague with all the evils which plague mankind. For Tarrou the real point is: can man fight plague with plague? Can he, in fighting the enemies of mankind, kill the enemies of mankind? He does not wish to be a "carrier of the plague." But the plague carries him off as it does the child and the priest. What then is the plague? It cannot be merely fascism or communism; it cannot be the ideologies, only, of mankind, which cause death and suffering; nor is it merely to be identified with the counterforce which the good man finds it necessary to apply in order to preserve his integrity. An analysis of even the most self-sacrificing and selfless action will show that it may cause suffering and death to others. No, the plague is the universal condition of man, it is the "thing" in the universe which is hostile to man. It is

Death. And so the relationship comes full circle: the prints of the German Renaissance artists Durer and Holbein, showed the plague merely as death. Man is alive: his enemy is death. Death takes multitudinous forms and shapes. But it is always there. *The Plague* is really concerned to show the ways men can rebel against death, knowing always that the rats will once again visit their "happy city." One can show his allegiance to life and hence his rebellion against death by fighting any effort man makes to cooperate with death. One can fight legalized executions, one can protest torture, one can demand justice. Any alliance man makes with death makes death more powerful, gives it meaning when it is meaningless. It is for this reason that man should protest tyranny, or suffering, or pain.

But death cannot be eradicated. The citizens of Oran are the citizens of life itself; the greatest affliction they suffer when visited by the plague is not fear but the sense of separation, the loneliness of exile, the pain of imprisonment. But if they are the citizens of life, from what are they separated? From the world itself. This is the absurd. They are all exiles and strangers. The kingdom of life which they long for is not theirs. How then can men survive and endure in this mutual and universal exile? By mutual love and tolerance, by the general acceptance of those common values which ordinary men hold, and by seeking and allowing others to seek happiness. If Paneloux and Tarrou die by the plague, if Rieux and Grand and Rambert survive, it is precisely because the latter only seek happiness, the former heroism. Before heroism the imperative, "Be happy," must be allowed its primacy. The mass of men only seek happiness; their values are predicated on this. It is, then, ordinary humanity which provides the criteria for what is just and unjust, for what is good and not good. It is of course the insistence on the prerogative of the ordinary values of humanity which marks the humanist of the West.

EDUCATION

The humanist has always attached what must seem, to those outside the tradition, extraordinary importance to education. The reason for this is that it is only through education that the system of ordinary values can be taught. Each man is a provincial in his own existence, each society provincial in its own time and space. Good intentions without the perspectives afforded by education can as easily lead to the destruction of human values as bad intentions. Education corrects sensibility and perspectives; it allows a view of differences, it shows limits, it insists upon one seeing that the world is complex, not simple, variable and full of possibilities, not single and narrow. But the education requested by Camus and the humanists is primarily an education in literature, not technology. Literature is always on the side of man and his ordinary human values; it sees the world as concrete and particular. Science handles the world by ignoring the specific; it always seeks general principles. To the writer the world is made up of single, individual elements, each precious; to the scientist the world is made up of systems, abstractions. All ideologies are scientific systems. Many use religions as if they were. Cottard in *The Plague* is unhappy because he is "an ignorant." He could have been "saved" if he had been "educated." He thinks that society is against him. There is no way he can join it, and therefore he turns against it. So Camus recommends education as the great safeguard of happiness. It teaches man his limits.

ESSAY QUESTIONS AND ANSWERS

Question: What is the significance of the two strange characters mentioned in *The Plague*: the draper who occupies his time transferring beans from one pot to another, and the old man who calls cats beneath his window for the sole purpose of spitting on them?

Answer: Camus is always and ever concerned with the need for tolerance of others no matter how odd they are, how strangely they occupy their own existence. The whole meaning of *The Stranger*, for instance, may be interpreted as a plea for tolerance. Meursault goes to his death, not so much because he murdered the Arab, but because he is different. The odd and ever grotesque characters in Camus' novels are there for a number of reasons: because he loved them and found them attractive as symbols of the infinite varieties of human beings, as representatives of the possible ways in which men may occupy the Sisyphusean task of dominating the absurd (occupied as they are purely meaningless gestures and activities), or as emblems of the fact that merely to be alive is enough. Some, like Rieux and Rambert and Grand and Paneloux, are occupied in what are generally accepted as "useful" occupations. But usefulness and uselessness are determined by purely human and hence relative standards. The old draper is alive; if he wishes to spend his life transferring beans from one pot to another, let him. He is not hurting anyone. Nor is the old man spitting on the cats. When the plague comes and all the cats are killed as possible carriers of the plague, the old man's reason for living is taken away from him. The reader will recall the little woman, "the robot" of *The Stranger*, meticulously ticking off her radio programs in the magazine, and Salamano and his dog. Meursault himself says he would have become accustomed to being confined in the trunk of a tree, so long as he could see the sky.

Question: What form does *The Plague* take?

Answer: Its form is that of a chronicle. A chronicle is the journal of an event as it occurs, day by day or time period by time period. It differs from a history proper in that it is usually contemporaneous with the events described or narrated. Ordinarily chronicles are the materials out of which histories are made. The historian, at a distance from the event described in the chronicle, is able to select, separate, and connect elements in the chronicle into what is to him a meaningful pattern. The chronicler theoretically has no means by which he is able to gauge the relative importance of events: the historian has. By calling his novel a chronicle Camus wishes to preserve the illusion of contemporaneity to the events narrated. This aids in assuring verisimilitude or the believability of his story. It also gives to it the air of specific time and place, which he desired. In spite of this it is not quite a true chronicle for the simple reason that Camus has ordered all the events, and the sequence of events, to ensure that each element will support the meaning of his novel.

Question: Why is Grand rather than Tarrou or Rieux the "hero" of *The Plague*?

Answer: It might be argued that Rieux or Tarrow is in fact the "hero." Let us consider these possibilities. Rieux does more, perhaps, than any other to meet the dangers of the plague and conquer it. He is always in the midst of it. He does his work loyally and dutifully. In this he meets Camus' requirements for the limited and relative duty to mankind. He hates evil and is consciously committed to fighting the plague as an evil to mankind. But he is not the hero. This may merely be because, out of modesty as the narrator, he cannot identify himself as such. But a better reason is that, in fact, in doing what he does, he is, commendable as it is, just doing his job. His vocation involves him in his actions. Tarrou, on the other hand, is carrying out a lifelong search for peace. He is a revolutionary. He too is committed to the fight against the plague. He desires the heroic dimensions of the saint of humanity. This very heroism prevents him from being the hero. The fact is that he is extraordinary. Grand, on the other hand, is ordinary. He fights the plague in the best way he can. He keeps exact records. His ordinariness would be questionable if he had been able to complete his novel. He is a clerk, not a high functionary of the local government. He could just as well have joined the "passive mass." and not become involved. But he does get involved. This involvement makes him the hero of the book.

Question: There is no villain in *The Plague*. Why?

Answer: There is no human villain in *The Plague* but there is a villain: it is the plague itself. It is for this very reason, however, that no character in *The Plague* is condemned. This lack of condemnation is both the moral strength and moral weakness of *The Plague*. Since all men are, by being men, on the side of life, none can be condemned. Rambert is not coerced by Rieux to stay. He is actively helped by Rieux in his preparations for escape. Nor is Cottard condemned. Nor is Father Paneloux. Nor even the "passive mass." How men choose to act in life cannot be held against them until such time as they become the instruments of death. If all men were educated to understand the situation in which man is, there would be no villains, none to condemn. To condemn is to imply that one is above the universal human condition. One may not judge another for the simple reason that no one is in possession of the absolute standard by which such a judgment could be carried out. Judges are absolutists: they believe that what in fact is relative is not relative. Camus constantly held that any absolute standard is unattainable. All we can ever hope to have is a general, limited, and relative standard which develops out of an understanding of ordinary human values and, while not violating them, ensures that they will be preserved. Therefore neither Camus nor his narrator Dr. Rieux can presume to judge or condemn.

ALBERT CAMUS

THE REBEL

. . . .

INTRODUCTION

Having accepted the absurd and demonstrated why suicide was an act of faithlessness to life, Camus went on to give a further expression of what can only be termed his "ethic" in "The Rebel." The basic proposition which "The Rebel" explores is, given the absurd, is murder justifiable? If it is, then the position he arrives at-that life is valuable for its own sake-in "The Myth of Sisyphus," is contradicted. It is also an analysis of the reasons the absurdist has for enduring. In this sense it goes beyond the first book, goes beyond justification for individual existence to a justification of all existence; from man to men, from the private suicide and nonsuicide to totalitarian mass extermination and their opponents, the "conquerors," or as he calls them, "the rebels."

If man decides to live, it means that there is value in living; rebellion itself is an act of faith in the value of life. But if life is valuable for the individual, it must also be valuable for all individuals. Rebellion to ensure the preservation of some value which cannot be denied, which is so valuable that to live without it people will die, is an affirmation of some irreducible element in existence which is not to be denied, for oneself or others. But the act of rebellion has a tendency to become absolute. The desire to ensure justice or freedom for oneself leads to revolution; and, as Camus demonstrates with lucid and inescapable logic, leads to more repressive forms of government, to totalitarian repressions of freedom in the name of ideologies. The question then is how to salvage the good of rebellion from the evil of revolution. All revolutionaries tend to be absolutist. They cease to be interested in personal justice, and they substitute notions of abstract justice. In the end they end up denying, implicitly or explicitly, the value of individual existence. So they do not hesitate to murder in order to carry out their solution. The fact that the deaths of others are justified by power, by expediency, by doctrine, by ideological conviction does not preclude the term "murder" from being supplied to those deaths. The perpetrators of these crimes are still culpable.

"The purpose of this essay," Camus says, "is once again to face the reality of the present . . .; it is an attempt to understand the times in which we live." And what sort of times do we live in? It is one in which, "in a space of fifty years, uproots, enslaves, or kills seventy million human beings. . . ." How did such a situation come about?

It is Camus' conviction that revolt is one of the "essential dimensions" of mankind. But the nature of this revolt has changed. The revolt of the slave against master, or those in poverty against those who have, is of the past. The revolt, from the eighteenth century on, is "**metaphysical**"; it is a revolt against the condition of existence itself. But the very revolt has its positive aspect; it denies a new unity and understanding of existence, a new synthesis and order.

From this point he reviews the history of this revolt; considering the case of Marquis de Sade who abhorred creation and desired its destruction, analyzing the position of the various Romantic rebels (Milton's Satan, Baudelaire, the cult of the "dandy," the insurrectionist poet), then passing on to others. But Camus is more interested in revolt as it takes a political form. He notes that all revolutions imply the establishment of a new government; rebellion on the other hand has no plan. The State born of revolution thirstily absorbs the freedom of individuals. The city of Marx, "the logical conclusion of inordinate . . . philosophical ambitions," in the last analysis, is "founded on terror"-on murder, on the implicit understanding that murder will be done.

What is Camus' answer to this seemingly blind alley at the end of the logic of rebellion and revolution? Man must recognize "limits" and "measures." He must recognize restraint as part of the condition of freedom. In all of us are the seeds of destruction and domination, especially active in those who recognize the absurd. "But our task is not to unleash them on the world; it is to fight them in ourselves and in others."

THE REBEL

First Camus addresses himself to the problem of defining what a rebel is. He is a man who, pushed up to or beyond a certain point, says "no." The point at which he says "no" affirms a recognition of limits. These limits bound the irreducible substance of his integrity, of his own notion of his untouchable, uncontrollable, uncommittable individuality. He does not wish to deny others their integrity; he merely wishes to establish his own. Characteristically, the rebel reaches a position of "all or nothing." He is willing to die, if necessary, for his demand. This leads, inevitably, to the notion that there is a "value" in his demand which transcends his individual "value." But this very characteristic of "all or nothing" has its bad effects as well as good. It leads, as Camus will show later, to the evils of totalitarian systems and ideologies. But rebellion in itself is good: "Rebellion, though apparently negative, since it creates nothing, is profoundly positive in that it reveals the part of man which must always be defended."

But rebellion, as such, seems to be limited to the Western world and to have accelerated in its activities during the last number of centuries. The reason for this is easy to find: rebellion is only possible in certain kinds of cultural situations, in certain types of social and political communities. The spirit which activates rebellion is possible only in a society where "theoretical equality conceals great factual inequalities." Such is the case only in Western culture. The rebel is the man who is on the point of rejecting the traditional, given "world" system for one conceived in his own terms, in terms of "reason." It would be possible to show that only two worlds exist: the "sacred world," where everything is given and accepted as given by higher authority; and the world of rebellion, where all such given values are resisted, fought against for the purpose of establishing one's own "human" rules and explanations. Today not only individuals but whole societies have wished to discard "the secret world." This is then the essential problem to be answered: "Is it possible to find a rule of conduct outside the realm of religion and its absolute values?" In order to find out if such a rule is possible it will be necessary to survey the various kinds of rebels and rebellion and see whether their answers offer us anything valuable for our inquiry.

METAPHYSICAL REBELLION

Rene Descartes, the seventeenth-century French philosopher, trying to establish a fundamental fact of existence on which to found his epistemology (theory of knowledge), arrived at the axiom Cogito ergo sum ("I think, therefore I am"). Rebellion for Camus is primal evidence of the same order. "I rebel-therefore we exist." Rebellion is communal, not solitary. Therefore the act of rebellion affirms not only the rebel's existence, but also the community's. **Metaphysical** rebellion is a protest against the whole creation itself. The rebellious slave rebels against his condition as a slave; the **metaphysical** rebel rebels against his condition as a man. The paradoxical quality of rebellion is that it affirms not only one's own existence but the existence of one's opponent or antagonist. Therefore the rebellion against God affirms the existence of God in the mind of the rebel. Camus calls the roll of those Greek rebels from Prometheus (who rebelled against Zeus) through Achilles and Oedipus and other Greek tragic figures. But at the basis of all these rebellions was not the belief that the gods were ranged against man. The point of Greek tragedy is to demonstrate the limits of existence, and to demonstrate the "measure" of man's fate. It is only with the appearance of the late Greek philosophers Epicurus and Lucretius that an activist rebellion against destiny and death appears. Both insist that the gods are indifferent to or ignorant of man's fate; therefore man should ignore the gods. Life is all he has. Life is his limit. By repudiating the gods they take the place of the gods themselves. But rebellion against such gods as filled the Greek pantheon is not a true **metaphysical** rebellion. The Greek gods did not create the world; they did not create man. Their essential difference from man was that they did not suffer and they did not die. Man needs a personal God, one who has created the world and mankind, before a true rebellion can take place. Otherwise "he" cannot be called to account.

Such a God was provided in the Judeo-Christian culture. Therefore real rebellion is possible only in this culture. Camus calls such rebels the children of Cain, the son of Adam who was the first murderer. While Christianity held the Western world together through the God-man Christ, rebellion was quieted. God had become man and taken on the total burden of human pain, suffering, and death. When, however, the rationalistic spirit began to reverse the name, and call Christ the man-God, the way was gradually opened to eliminate Christ as God from consideration. This led to a free confrontation between the rebel and God. The abyss separating man and God was reopened. In the centuries preceding the eighteenth and its open rebellion against heaven, free thinkers had done all they could to turn Christ into an innocent victim of an outrageous God.

NEGATIONS

The first "coherent" rebellion of the **metaphysical** kind is offered by de Sade. His negation is the most extreme. Most of his life he spent in prison. He wrote prodigiously. Absent, so to speak, from reality, his position was pushed to the extreme. He denied creation, hated it, would destroy it. His enemy was God and God's creation. Actually he wished to substitute himself for God. Murder of course was not merely allowed; it was demanded. God oppresses and denies mankind; de Sade oppresses and denies God. For de Sade whatever is evil is good. He makes a total and point-by-point replacement of the tenets of the Judeo-Christian system with their opposites. But to exalt de Sade, as some have done, as the philosopher in chains, as a new Prometheus, is to misread him. Far from desiring to help mankind, he abhors it and wishes its destruction. From his total negativism we can learn nothing of a system of values, or "rule of conduct" drawn from the human condition itself. De Sade ends up taking all the power into his own hands. He is the archetype of the absolute dictator. "Two centuries ahead of his time de Sade extolled totalitarian societies in the name of unbridled freedom. . . ," and this, rebellion does not demand.

Camus next considers those interesting phenomena of the eighteenth and early nineteenth centuries who go by the collective name of the "dandies." For the most part, in France, literary men, especially poets, they struck the pose of rebellion, allied themselves with Lucifer, and said with him "non serviam" ("I will not serve"). They sought their models in the position of revolt in Milton's Satan (in *Paradise Lost*), in the romantic heroes of the English poet Byron, those handsome, lost, proud devils suffering from unrequited and unrequitable love, in Shelley's lust for the impossible infinite. Their style of life they took from Beau Brummell; their philosophy they took from Baudelaire. They were lost; they knew it, they gloried in it. It was their badge of honor. So they dressed in fantastic clothes and said and did outrageous things to shock the bourgeoisie. They held opinions for which they hoped they would suffer. Some did. Not most. The capacity of any generation to be shocked is limited: the capacity to imagine shocking things is also limited. Most "dandies" end up being merely narcissistic. Their contribution to humanity is small: a few new articles of male clothing, the word "dandy," a few excellent poems, and an incalculable supply of rather childish displays of temper couched in execrable verse. There is one thing, however, to be said for the concept of the dandy. It supplied, by its implication that each man, living in an absurd world, should make his own role, should create himself as a work of art, a way of existence, a style of life.

DOSTOEVSKY

The dandy needs God in order to exist as a dandy. His relationship to God is a type of "flirtation." In Ivan Karamazov of Dostoevsky, the rebellion is of a more profound kind. Because Karamazov insists on man's innocence and his unjust punishment, his indictment is moral. If evil is essential to creation, "then creation is unacceptable." Therefore Ivan will go beyond God for his guiding principle-to justice. In doing this, according to Camus, Ivan takes the necessary step out of the "sacred world" into the "rebellious world." Out of the human condition itself he attempts to create the tenets of faith, the rule of conduct. Ivan will "live" even without knowing why. But having arrived at nihilism Ivan states: "Everything is permitted." But Ivan himself recognizes that there is a contradiction here: if everything is permitted, then justice is denied. The Grand Inquisitor is the type of the nihilist who creates a new order of justice which ends up being unjust. It murders in the name of its justice. Ivan goes mad, a kind of suicide.

AFFIRMATIONS

The German philosopher Nietzsche is the first to face the absurd and, having denied God, and therefore the sanctions for moral behavior which derive from His existence, to set out to create a moral order derived exclusively from human existence itself. Nietzsche, Camus says, "will deliver the world." He was the first to recognize nihilism, and attempted to avoid the cataclysm of the future which he discerned nihilism would bring about. Can one live, asks Nietzsche, believing in nothing? Yes, he cries. Accepting nihilism, man must create a new law out of himself. In *The Will to Power*, Nietzsche denounces the "calumniators of the world," and demands that the world be accepted. He constructs his philosophy "on rebellion." Man is alone in the world, masterless. Freedom is the acceptance of obligations. Chaos is servitude. To live in a lawless world is impossible. Life implies law.

Comment

Nietzsche's philosophy of the need for rule and order as a necessary condition of existence was later used as a justification of the New Order of Hitler. It was carried to monstrous ends by the Nazis. But, says Camus (and others), the Nazis distorted Nietzsche. It is hard to find in the history of intelligence a man who has been so unjustly treated: "We shall never finish making reparation for the injustice done to him" in making him "the master of lies and violence."

OTHER LITERARY REBELS

Camus next considers other rebels, especially poets such as Lautreamont, Rimbaud, and the Surrealists. All desired the overthrow of society, all were affronted by the meaninglessness of existence. In Lautreamont we find an interesting archetype of the failed rebel. *The Songs of Maldoror*, the poet's first book, is a long hymn of revolt; Poesies is a catechism of conformity. This is brought about by the nature of rebellion itself: all or nothing. The rebel who demands the absolute grows weary of the psychic tension demanded of such a stance and swings back the same distance in the opposite direction; here he finds himself not in the position of the rebel anymore but settled into the solidifying mud of established tradition. There is always the danger that the rebel will rebel against the rebellion. The same paradox is illustrated by the Russians revolutionists who, nursed in their fiery youth on the firewater of anarchism, in time sobered up and settled joyfully into the Alcoholics Anonymous of Communist discipline. In art, in philosophy, in politics, the lust for the absolute leads to the destruction of revolt.

POLITICS

Camus' primary concern in "The Rebel" is to analyze the present. The present is, for him, overwhelmingly committed to political revolution. Therefore, now he turns his attention to politics, and revolution. Camus' position is clearly on record. It is the position which "The Rebel" will again offer as its conclusion: "the only revolution which is adjusted to the measure of man is to be found in the acceptance of relative aims and ambitions, which means fidelity to the human lot."

The French Revolution was betrayed by its oversimplifying doctrinaire fanatics who did not consider the complexity of man. All criticism was suppressed because they could not believe that their opponents might have a point. It is with Hegel, however, that the modern ideologies which derive their sanctions only from history begin. All values otherwise sanctioned are destroyed. Hegel postulates an Absolute which will be realized only when the process we call History ends. This Idea, delivered like an egg from the end of the long funnel of process, is the criterion and canon, the object of worship, the measure of right and wrong, of what is just and unjust. The individual is less important than the State, which is the "Church" of this Idea. He must serve the Idea. Eventually of course, the individual ceases to be important at all. The State is important. Those who hinder the realization of the State are to be cut out like cancers. Thus murder is sanctioned.

All modern forms of totalitarianism derive from Hegel, implicitly or explicitly. Under his influence, in the atmosphere of thought his philosophy created, ideology becomes prophetic. It ceases to regard the present as important except as a stage toward the future. The future becomes the only true reality. All must serve it. So the revolutions of the Right and the Left, fascism and communism, become identical in their disregard for life, for freedom, for individual integrity. The rebel has become the tyrant. And against this tyrant, the individual, always concerned with establishing the limits, the irreducible substance, of his person which is valuable to him, must rebel.

CONCLUSIONS

Camus, having surveyed the nature of the rebel, having analyzed its various forms, and gone on to show why the modern revolutions have failed, makes unmistakable his belief that modern European and Western man has gone through a series of stages paralleling physical growth. His initial rebellion ended in the childish tantrums of de Sade and the preadolescent attitudinizing of the dandies, then went on to end in the savage clubs and gangs of adolescence with all their intolerance of the outsider. He hopes that the terrible cataclysms, the horrors and pain and death which resulted from this adolescent fury will have nudged humanity into adulthood. Man has freed himself from the father, and has used his freedom only to destroy. Now the demands of maturity insist that he be responsible about his freedom. Maturity demands **realism**: realism inculcates the virtues of moderation. Man must seek the measure, the harmony, the order, which will ensure his own freedom and integrity but also the freedom and integrity of others, of all: "All can live again by the side of those who sacrificed themselves in

1905 [a reference to the Russian revolutionaries of that time who sacrificed themselves by consenting to pay with their lives for the lives they took, thus recognizing the limits of the possible], but on condition that they understand that they correct one another, and that there is, under the sun, a limit which controls them all." No man is God. This is the beginning of a mature politics.

Comment

Camus is a liberal humanist. His position is not radically or even greatly different from the position of that long line of Western humanists who always insisted on the necessity of protecting human integrity. It is a list which includes many of the great philosophers and fathers of the Christian tradition; it includes many of the greatest thinkers of the Renaissance, both in and out of the Church. And the ranks of such humanists has been swelled prodigiously during this last century. Camus, in "The Rebel," offers a consistent and coherent criticism of ideology from the liberal humanist's standpoint. In the vigor, thoroughness, and lucidity of this criticism, the full articulation of the tenets of this faith, Camus moves to the front rank and becomes a spokesman. His great importance for our time is that he constructs an ethical system of great subtlety and persuasiveness out of the context of the human situation itself, without appealing to a priori (or given) principles. In this sense, and perhaps in this sense only, he is an existentialist; out of existence itself he draws the axioms by which existence should be realized. He differs, certainly, from Sartre, who says that although man recognizes the absurdity and meaningless of existence, he should impose meaning, more or less arbitrarily, by committing himself to a cause, engage himself in a system which, by a suspension of disbelief, he accepts as valid. The difference between Camus and

Sartre is the difference between a man joyfully swimming in his element and a man standing just in up to his knees, shivering, with crouched shoulders and clenched teeth; he is at the beach and he has to participate in what is expected of him.

Fundamentally Camus tries to get back to the relationship which primitive peoples have to the earth and nature. He, of course, recognized the incredible difficulties which modern sensibilities have in trying to reach this kind of total rapport. Modern man has the baggage of thousands of years of intelligence and reason to deal with. One can suggest that man merely fling all this baggage overboard: the result of this abandonment is often only revolting, not revolt. License is, as many have said, not liberty. This is why Camus insists on the necessary combination of lucidity and freedom. Lucidity shows us that nothing operates well unless it acknowledges its own limits. The aerialist in his acrobatic freedom knows precisely the limits of his ability within the boundaries set by gravity; the composer knows the proper limits of the instruments of the orchestra in relationship to each other, or else what he composes will not work. Many ideologies, Camus says, fail in the same way that the composition of an insufficiently aware composer fails, or a poorly trained acrobat. One who orchestrates for society needs to know the multitudinous complexities of society and man in society. He needs to know the limits of the inherent conditions of existence. Harmony will never be produced except by knowing such limits.

The romanticist sees himself as the single instrument; that is why inevitably he begins to resemble God and inevitably to take on the attributes and characteristics of absolute power. Maturity is the understanding that one is part of an immense continuum, a piece of the unbroken fabric of total existence. The preservation of one's own integrity them implies, demands, the preservation of the integrity of others. A totalitarian ideology is like a cancerous growth in the body. It insists that all other cells of the body become like itself or die. Of course, the whole organism dies or suffers terrible pain. So society during the last hundred years has been suffering the pains of ideological cancer. And, in spite of the major surgery of the last two wars, the cancer cells are still with us. A healthy body is one in which all the cells acknowledge the integrity of all other cells; the result is an orchestrated harmony, an order, which we recognize as good health. This kind of health is what Camus desires for the body of humanity.

The Greeks had a saying which (in its Latin form) sums up an essential part of Camus' politics: means sana in corpore sano-"a healthy mind in a healthy body." They had another consistent with this: "nothing in excess." Although these sayings do not exhaust Camus' recommendations, they point us in the proper direction for understanding them. A healthy mind is harmonious because it realizes its limits; it is not fanatical or excessive. So with a healthy body. What modern politics needs to do is return to these ancient Greek principles, and direct man's existence by them. Disease is always an excess of some sort. An excess of justice leads to tyranny; an excess of tolerance leads to intolerance; an excess of mercy leads to injustice. The mature mind sees that this is true. The perfect society is one in which all are capable of assuming their perfect and complete dimensions without distorting the dimensions or limiting the perfections of others. whatever makes for that society is good, whatever makes against that society is bad. The rebel is always necessary because we live in a world of men; and men will always have in them the impulse to expand their own freedom at the expense of the freedom of others. Against such impulses the rebel must always be on guard.

It is obvious that in his last great philosophical work Camus was working towards a comprehensive system of ethics which he hoped would serve a world beyond nihilism. Starting not from traditional principles, but out of principles evolved from his own personal and concrete experiences, he constructed a system which resembles that of Aristotle. Accept nothing, setting aside all the systems which had evolved during the last thousands of years, he looked upon existence with virgin eye, and by the purity of his conscience and the rigor and refinement of his sensibility made a valuable contribution to man's knowledge of himself and his predicament. Even those who do not share in his basic assumption that human existence is incomprehensible can learn a great deal from such integrity. And besides, there are certain implications some have discerned in the later works of Camus which seem to suggest that he was moving towards a position beyond absurdity, that he was in fact beginning to see a transcendent significance in human existence and the human condition. Nor would those who have closely followed the development of his mind have been shocked by this.

ESSAY QUESTIONS AND ANSWERS

Question: What is Camus' definition of the rebel?

Answer: The rebel is he who says "no." He says "no" because he has seen the limits to which he will allow something precious and irreducible in him to be dominated by others. There are varieties of rebels: the slave, the servant, the creation. The slave rebels against another man; the servant (all those used the poor, for instance) rebel against the classes which use them; the creation rebels against his creator (**Metaphysical** rebellion).

Question: What is the difference between the rebellion and revolution?

Answer: The rebel has no plan or program beyond establishing his integrity. A rebellion is staged to redress an imbalance, to re-establish an order in which the rebel regains and keeps his integrity. A revolutionary has a plan and program. It is ordinarily of the all-or-nothing variety. He wishes to overthrow the existing order of things and replace it with his own order. His all-or-nothing attitude leads to intolerance, repression, and eradication of differences. The difference between rebellion and revolution is the difference between what is good and what is bad in recent history.

Question: What importance has Hegel in the philosophy of Camus?

Answer: It is in Hegel's notion of the transcendent notion of the "Spirit of History" (the Absolute which was the "purpose" of history [human existence]) that Camus locates the bad example which changed Marx from an empirical analyst of society to a "prophet." The "prophet" looks beyond present existence for its meaning. When Marx pointed out a distant point in the future towards which history should strive, he opened the Pandora's box of evil which sanctions repression. mindless discipline, and murder "for the greater good." This has the effect of debasing individuals, and eventually ignoring them. Man becomes not a slave of another man, but a slave of the future, not a creature of God, but a creature of the State. In all ideologies, man is used as a tool, as a means; but, insists Camus, he is an end in himself.

Question: What significance does the notion of "measure" have in Camus' philosophy?

Answer: The notion of "measure" is of supreme importance in Camus' philosophy. It sums up the essence of what he asks in the present time, the time of revolution. By "measure" is meant that attitude of mind just the contrary of "all or nothing." The realist is a man who understands reality as it is, not as he wishes it to be. Better still, the realist is one who maintains at the same time a knowledge of what reality is and what it can be. He, in brief, recognizes limits. He understands that freedom for an entity is the full exercise of that entity's powers within its own proper limits. All modern revolutions have failed because of excess. Excess is caused by a lack of "measure." The notion is similar to Aristotle's principle of justice. Measure is justice. Anyone who has attempted to sing in a chorus in which everyone went his own way will recognize what happens when there is no sense of "measure." And yet a chorus in which the individual voice capacities and differences are ignored is not going to function very well either. Measure is the total orchestration of all the parts which results only when the individual integrity of each part is realized.

Question: In what way is Camus an existentialist?

Answer: It is common practice to lump together a whole group of modern writers, especially French, as existentialists and attribute to them common characteristics and principles. Such categorizing is sloppy and, more than that, false. Technically an existentialist is one who believes that the primary data of knowledge is deprived from "existence" itself. In this sense St. Thomas, the great Scholastic theologian and philosopher, is an existentialist: "Nihil est in intellectu nisi quam primum in sensum" (Nothing is in the intellect unless it is first in the senses"). Most poets and novelists are, by the nature of their talents, existentialists. Nothing is "real" which does not grow out of, or locate itself, in the visible. This by no means implies that the invisible is not real. The emotions, thought itself, is not visible, yet these are real. There are a group of modern philosophers who are atheistic existentialists. Their existential stance grows out of nihilism. Of these Sartre is one. Denying God, eliminating any transcendental meaning to human existence, they derive their philosophy from existence and limit it to existence. Camus is also one of these. However, he parts company from Sartre in that his existentialism is positive, whereas Sartre's has remained negative. Camus says that although existence is meaningless by an a priori or transcendent standard, it is completely meaningful to those who accept it as is. For Sartre the recognition of meaninglessness leads to nausea; man is stranger, an accidental awareness in existence. For Camus man is, for whatever reason, part of existence. Not nausea but joy should his portion.

Question: What relationship have "The Myth of Sisyphus" and "The Rebel" to one another?

Answer: The relationship is close and consistent. "The Myth of Sisyphus" concentrates on the individual. "The Rebel" concentrates on the community, or the interrelationships of individuals. They both start from the assumption that existence is meaningless. "The Myth of Sisyphus" takes as its thesis the justification for continuing to live in an absurd universe. It establishes the reasons why suicide is wrong, given the absurd. "The Rebel" takes as its thesis the justification for an ordered and harmonious society. Specifically it is concerned with whether murder is justified. At this point the two theses are shown to be closely rooted in the same principle. If suicide is wrong because life is in itself valuable, murder is wrong for the same reason: life, one's own, and others, is valuable. Life is in itself valuable: this is the foundation of Camus' entire philosophy. His ethical system derives entirely from this simple concept.

Question: Does Camus believe that revolution is the unending condition of man?

Answer: By no means. There are cultures in which revolutions never took place, and times in which revolution need not take place. If he concerns himself so much with revolt and revolution it is because these are the times of revolution. He is primarily concerned with analyzing this present time, which needs explanation. The condition of revolution only occurs when the dichotomy between what ought to be and what is enrages a large number of men in society and they try to reverse the situation. Such conditions seem to be limited to the Western world. A change of government is not in itself a revolution.

Question: Does this mean that the type of the rebel will disappear because he has no function?

Answer: Given the impulses of men to cause an imbalance in society by greed, or ambition, or ignorance, or evil, the rebel will never disappear. His presence will no doubt always be necessary. In a sense, he will always be the conscience of his times, a device to measure the presence of intolerance and tyranny. In the precarious boat in which mankind rows he will always be required to say "stop, you're rocking the boat" or "move over," or "pull your oar with the rest." In the sense in which he uses the term, Camus was himself the constant rebel of his time, who took upon himself the never ending task of pointing out the excesses which destroy the harmony of humanity.

ALBERT CAMUS

Camus' novel *The Fall* is called in French *La Chute*. Both titles must be considered to assume the full symbolic weight the book carries. *The Fall* of course, is dense with significances for the Western World and its Judeo-Christian tradition. Adam, the first man, fell from his relationship to God through his sin of disobedience, the primal crime. This "fall" brought death and suffering and pain into the world. St. Augustine, like Camus an African, called Adam's fall "O, felix culpa" ("oh, happy fall") because without it man would not have had the visitation of Christ and the life beyond this life in Paradise. But the French title, *La Chute*, has its own significance. One of the meanings of "La Chute" is the "tunnel." It is this which allows Camus to make use of Dante's geography and cosmology in *The Divine Comedy* for his own purposes. Dante, like *Alice in Wonderland*, led not by the rabbit but by Vergil, descends into hell through a tunnel. His purpose is to find himself. In this he was following the ancient Greek dictum: know thyself. To know oneself involves the terrible process of stripping off layers and layers of deceit. It is the process through which Oedipus goes in Sophocles' play *Oedipus Rex*. It is, in a sense, parallel to the process of psychoanalysis.

But Camus' hero Clamence is, as Camus says, a comic reaction. He is certainly meant to be a kind of self-portrait. But there is a distinction to be made; it is not, one believes, a portrait as Camus believed himself to be, but as his detractors believed him to be. The novel is concerned with guilt. Clamence, an ex-judge, is living in a self-imposed exile in Amsterdam, Holland. Around him the canals form circle after circle, in obvious analogy to the circles of Dante's Hell. The atmosphere is dank, musty, and mysterious. Clamence tells his story to a nameless listener who he has cornered in one of Amsterdam's bars. The listener is of course the reader. What is Clamence's crime? One night, crossing one of the many bridges of Paris, he had heard a woman sobbing, and later, the splash as her body hit the water. He had ignored her. Later this memory begins to prey on his mind. He sees himself as bearing the burden of guilt for her suffering and suicide. So now, no longer able to function as a judge, he has come to live in Amsterdam, his mission being to tell his story and convince others that they are equally guilty.

If we identify Camus with this character it would be possible to say that he was beginning to move towards a traditional Christian belief in the guilt of all men, or even that he was accepting the common liberal position that all men are guilty for the unhappiness of others. But this reading overlooks one essential fact of *The Fall*. Clamence is, unmistakably, a comic creation. It is difficult to believe that Camus would have couched such a serious change of position as a conversion to Christianity in such a thoroughly ironic testament. The fact is that Camus does not accept Clamence's guilt at all. Clamence, after all, is trying to destroy the happiness that many people have earned by their commitment to ordinary human values. He wishes to stain the glass, heap even on the innocent the burden of guilt which, Camus logically believes, they have not earned. In fact, he was really criticizing a certain liberal immolation in the guilt which results when one has survived when others die. The Europe of the postwar period was full of this feeling. People demanded that Camus feel it. He rebelled. *The Fall* is his rebellion.

EXILE AND THE KINGDOM

In this book of short stories, published in 1957, Camus has moved into a new area. Here the readers feels the joy of creation, not so much at the service of philosophy, as at the service of creativeness. The settings are enlarged to include Brazil as well as France and North Africa. Camus himself said that these short stories were exercises in techniques in preparation for a new novel (probably *The First Man*). If so, this very concentration on techniques has provided Camus with a new freedom of tone and subject matter. These six stories are without significant political or even metaphysical meaning. They may be enjoyed simply for their art; significantly the reader does not enjoy the men and women in them for what they represent but for what they are.

In "The Woman Taken in Adultery," Janine longs for the freedom of the desert. The desert is symbolic (as it is in Balzac's famous short story "A Passion in the Desert") of the "kingdom" from which she has been exiled. She escapes into it, throwing off her commitments to civilization. Like Meursault at the end of his life, she feels "the tender indifference" of existence. Her adultery is, in fact, an adultery with this "indifferent" nature. Her "Nuptials" are just the ones which the inhuman systematization of civilization will not allow. Meursault's "mistress" is just Marie to him. "L'abstraction" is the great evil which men must always rebel against. In "The Confused Spirit" a missionary heroically, blindly, and absolutely devoted to Christianity has gone out among a savage tribe of North Africa to convert them. Castrated,

THE STRANGER AND OTHER WORKS

his tongue cut out, he has learned to worship their savage god Ra with the same absolute devotion. Now he waits to kill a new missionary who is on his way to the tribe. The absolutist, says Camus, is absolute in whatever situation he finds himself. The revolutionary who sets out to free man devotes himself with the same fanatical energy to binding him. But instead of arriving at his intellectual positions first and then creating characters who will represent them, Camus, in *Exile and the Kingdom*, invents characters in certain situations. Their vitality and energy carry themselves first, their meanings second. The reader is advised to start his reading of Camus with *Exile and the Kingdom*.

REVIEW OF CRITICISM

Camus And The Critics

When Camus published *The Stranger* and "The Myth of Sisyphus" in 1942, he became, almost overnight, one of France's best-known literary figures. His reputation continued to grow steadily throughout the world until in 1960 the Committee of the Swedish Academy awarded him what is acknowledged to be the most important accolade a writer can receive, the Nobel Prize for Literature. His death shortly after, it is generally believed, cut short a creative resurgence which was beginning to show signs of moving in a different direction. What those unfinished or unwritten works would have added to Camus' stature is impossible to estimate. Camus' work is complete. What remains now is to survey the growth of his reputation and summarize the attitudes various critics have had towards it. Because *The Stranger* appeared only twenty-three years ago, the body of criticism cannot necessarily be as large nor, for that matter, as diverse as it is for older writers of equal or even lesser importance.

Criticism In English

Fortunately the student has available the collection of critical essays gathered together by Germaine Bree (see Bibliography) that affords him, in one volume, most of the important essays which have been published on Camus. There is also Bree's own full-length critical analysis of the writer (see Bibliography) and the study-again full length-published by Philip Thody (see Bibliography). Other articles and books are listed in the Bibliography. In this section, all the essays discussed are to be found in the collection edited by Bree.

The Reputation Of Camus In America

In his excellent article "Camus in America" Serge Doubrovsky analyzes the reasons why Camus has appealed so strongly to Americans. He is, says Doubrovsky, the one writer who "attacks the problems of our time in depth." With Faulkner and Hemingway and the writers of their generation now gone, a vacuum was created. Camus alone filled that vacuum. Camus offered the reader characters sufficiently free of national characteristics and local peculiarities so that non-Algerians, non-Frenchmen, non-Europeans could identify with them. Sartre's characters, on the other hand, are felt as slightly alien; they are phenomena of France in a certain period and are thus limited. Americans are able to share with Camus his concern "for man's struggle within the universe and against it." In this he is easily assimilated into the tradition of the essential American novels, Melville, Hemingway. The very classlessness of America, which, in spite of multiple differences of interests, produces in most Americans a sense of unity against the common enemy, allows Americans to understand Camus' conception of the "plague" as a universal negating force to be fought by all. Sartre's demand that the plague be identified with totalitarianism of the Right, or with capitalism, limits his appeal and demonstrates Camus' wider range. The Americans also agree fundamentally with Camus' notion of the provisional victory for mankind against the "plague." The Americans are a people entirely "oriented toward this earth, fiercely resolved to make it produce everything it can for man." It is this aspect of America which finds in Camus a voice. He has expressed "in black and white the secular ethics which is at the heart of this American civilization. . . ."

O'Brien

Justin O'Brien, who has translated much of Camus into English, sees Camus' force in his moral militancy. In his essay "Albert Camus: Militant," O'Brien praises the author for seeing that "the era of the chair bound artists is over," and acting upon this belief. His activist part in the French Resistance gave him the right to speak out. His newspaper articles (collected in Actuelles, 1950, 1953, and 1958) "gave the postwar generation the moral guidance it seemed to need." It was his lucidity and courage, his lack of fear in speaking out on any "questions that torment us," which gave Camus the "personal equilibrium, without which his novels and plays would not be the consummate works of art they are." O'Brien puts Camus in the company of Pascal, La Bruyere, and Voltaire. His conscience was cleared by his courage; when he speaks we can trust what he says.

Sheed

Wilfred Sheed carries on the analysis of Camus as "the conscience of his generation." In spite of the danger that persons so called often begin to believe their own publicity and end up being "priggish, preachy and mechanically compassionate," Camus has avoided that danger. He has remained lucid and clear. The test was the Algerian war, in which emotion ran high, when people became partisans of one side or another and ended up praising the very acts of horror on their side as they condemned on the other. But Camus was consistent with his philosophical and ethical positions; he kept a clear head when others became irrational through passion. He said "we must condemn with equal force and in no uncertain terms the terrorism" applied by both sides. ". . . French opinion vaguely holds that the Arabs have in a way earned the right to slaughter and mutilate . . ." and "to justify himself, each relies on the other's crime." But Camus condemns both. This is common sense-from a distance. It is an indication of Camus' moral courage that he shows such common sense in the midst of the mob demanding that he take one side or the other. It is for this reason that Christians find in Camus a "chivalrous opponent," a man who is concerned with the right, not with being right.

Camus And Sartre

From the very beginning of Camus' emergence as a figure of French literary importance, his name was joined with Sartre's. In the popular mind they were lumped together as philosophers of the absurd. Their productions took parallel forms: books of philosophy, novels, plays, short stories, constant streams of articles. They became, in the eyes of the world, indisputably the two most important writers to come out of France during and after the war. Besides this the two men were close friends. It was Sartre's article on *The Stranger* called "An Explication of *The Stranger*" that was the first to show its great importance and to relate it specifically to "The Myth of Sisyphus." Sartre, as a formally trained and original philosopher, was instrumental in analyzing Camus' thought in terms of philosophical tradition. As an intellectual who had already established a reputation for himself in France, he was also Camus' sponsor in French intellectual circles. It was then, a gauge of Camus' independence as a writer that he broke with Sartre, not by choice, but because his integrity led him away from Camus' political position. Sartre's side of the affair is to be found in Situations in the article "Reply to Camus," Camus' in Nicola Chiaromonte's article "Sartre versus Camus: A Political Quarrel," published in *Partisan Review* in 1952.

Origins Of The Quarrel

The specific cause of the quarrel was Camus' second philosophical essay, "The Rebel." The reader will recall that the essay was specifically concerned with whether anything justifies murder. It was Camus' position that nothing justifies murder. He analyzed how rebellion moves to revolution, pointing out that the rebel never has a program but merely wishes to restore a balance in which men can be happy. The revolutionary has a program. He wishes to replace the government. The program is an expression of his ideology. Since the ideology is almost always of the "all or nothing" variety, he justifies murder, assassination, torture, imprisonment to bring his program into being. This leads Camus to condemn communism as well as fascism. It was this condemnation of communism which led Sartre to quarrel with Camus. Sartre, although not a Communist and often outspoken in his criticism of many of its features, has, consistent with his notion of "engagement," come to support its programs. I say, "consistent with his notion of 'engagement,'" What does this mean? Sartre's "absurdity," unlike Camus', had led him to the position that the world was not only incomprehensible (which Camus agreed with) but meaningless (which Camus denied).

How could the world be made meaningful? Man, arbitrarily, imposes meaning. He becomes "engaged" by an act of the will. This accounts for Sartre's support of the Communist ideology without becoming a Communist.

Results Of The Quarrel

When Camus condemned communism, specifically since it had recently been disclosed that the Communists supported a great system of slave labor and concentration camps, Sartre broke with him. He believed, as Camus did not, that the "society of the future" justified the terror and crime of the present. This, of course, goes completely contrary to Camus' demand that it is the present life which must be preserved and given reverence. Nothing justifies murder. Camus did not reply to Sartre. Like Meursault he believed in the value of silence, especially since he had already made his position plain. If he made any answer it is to be found in *The Fall*. It is probably true, however, that Camus was pained by Sartre's attack, not merely because it came from a friend, but because it demonstrated that even the incredible intelligence of a man like Sartre was subject to the "plague." It showed how precarious was the balance in which "ordinary human values" are preserved.

Chiaromonte's Reply

Camus' justification is to be found in Chiaromonte's article, already noted. Chiaromonte shows the fundamental suicidal tendency of Sartre's thought, especially in Sartre's belief (held, apparently with some joy) that when the revolution succeeds, he (Sartre) and his kind would be the first to be eliminated. This clearly demonstrates the essential negation at the heart of Sartre's philosophy and the positive strength of Camus' philosophy. In fact Sartre had never moved beyond the position of the nihilist. Unconsciously his tradition of rationalism had led him to impose a meaning on existence which in his heart he did not believe was there. His "engagement" is merely a therapeutic device for preserving himself from suicide in the midst of a lifelong "nausea." He never understood that given nihilism there are only two logical positions which can be taken: suicide or acceptance of life as meaningful in itself. But if life is meaningful in itself, all life is meaningful. If all life is meaningful, then murder, for any cause, can never be justified. In a secular world it is to Camus man must turn if he is to endure, not to Sartre.

Camus And Algeria

Roger Quilliot, in his essay "Albert Camus' Algeria," shows the constant of Camus' birthplace to the work. The setting of *The Fall* in Amsterdam, for instance, reinforces the symbol of that city as hell for Camus. There is no sun. It is the primitive, sun-drenched, sensual world of his childhood which feeds Camus in his philosophy, in his creative life: that is, his mind and his imagination. In Algeria he knew the equilibrium between life and death which he wished for all men. The plague comes from Europe. Europe's tendency to excess is what is wrong. In Algeria there is moderation; the rhythm of life includes all because it recognizes limits. It shares with the Greeks that temperament which recognizes that anything carried to an extreme is dangerous and leads to the upsetting of the balance of life. In Algeria too Camus had learned that the true kingdom of man, the exile, is the earth. It is European thought which has separated man from his true kingdom. The tendency towards fanaticism is, at root, caused by man's sense of dislocation and divorce from his true kingdom. Anyone who wishes to know Camus must understand the importance of his birthplace in this thought.

Camus And Religion

Many critics have judged Camus to be essentially concerned with religious problems: who is man, how should he live, what is his destiny, by what rules should be conduct himself? "In fact," says Thomas Hanna, in his article "Albert Camus and the Christian Faith," "it readily becomes apparent that in all his literary pieces Camus is centrally concerned with religious-moral **themes** . . .' and "Albert Camus is today's most articulate non-Christian thinker." Note that Camus is not an anti-Christian but "simply a non-Christian." It is with the Christian faith that Camus must come to terms. Camus believes that Christianity has been turned into "a doctrine of injustice." Christ was an innocent and unjustly killed. Christianity is founded on the acceptance of this injustice. The problems settled by the acceptance of the death of Christ are precisely the problems of evil and death. Accepting the innocent death of Christ means accepting evil and death. But these are precisely what the rebel cannot accept. The death of the innocent poses the essential problem. Father Paneloux in *The Plague* sees that the Christian must accept "the all or nothing" of his commitment to his faith. The equilibrium between humanity and nature was first broken by Christianity, which put man's salvation beyond nature. Camus' whole effort is to validate values drawn only out of man's relationship with nature. Because of the lucidity and integrity and consistency of his views Camus becomes a critic of Christianity whom the Christian can find valuable for the inspection of his own position.

Father Bernard Murchland, in his article "Albert Camus: The Dark Night Before the Coming of Grace?" goes even further.

He suggests that during the period just before his death Camus was moving steadily towards conversion to Roman Catholicism. The extreme logical integrity of Camus' conscience supports this belief. His art, towards the end, becomes "more serene, disinterested and assumes something comparable to a redemptive dimension." In *The Plague* he had been primarily concerned with serving men, not saving them. In *The Fall* and in *Exile and the Kingdom*, "he stresses the new values of penance and expiation" (however, for another view, see Thody's analysis of *The Fall* in his book listed in the Bibliography). Murchland takes the **irony** of *The Fall* into consideration. Camus' work has shown his "pilgrimage" out of absurdity toward a "high sense of purpose." It would not be surprising to see him finally adopt a position in which existence became "purposeful."

Henri Peyre, however, in his article "Camus the Pagan" insists that Camus was a pagan from first to last, and that there is no justification for seeing him as an inverted Christian moving towards conversion. Peyre sees Camus' value precisely in his thoroughgoing paganism. He quotes him as saying that "Contemporary unbelief does not rest on science. . . . It is a passionate unbelief." The evolution of Camus' ethics, from this position, is detailed in another article by Doubrovsky called "The Ethics of Albert Camus." Philip Thody analyzes the work of Camus as it moves from a personalist philosophy created out of a concrete situation into the great mainstream of liberal "humanism."

Camus In England

The British reputation of Camus is summarized by S. Beynon John in "Albert Camus: A British View." The British because of their distrust of abstraction have always found Camus' novels

BRIGHT NOTES STUDY GUIDE

more worthwhile than his philosophical essays. The novels are concrete and specific. John criticizes negatively the tendency of Camus to be abstract and overintellectualized, especially in his plays, although this tendency also weakens the characterizations in his novels and stories. His fiction is seen as a "deliberate transposition" of what are essentially intellectual conclusions into imaginative form. The transposition is not complete, and hence his characters never achieve the density and vitality of, say, Shakespeare or Dickens. Three "factors inhibit the sense of life in Camus' fiction . . .: the appeal to negation, the polytheistic experience of nature, and the force of abstraction." Even though Camus goes beyond negation, he retains "the negative cast of mind that the encounter with nihilism had engendered." Because his thought is "centered on death," his "rendering" of life is affected. He can experience "the vitality of what is diffused and collective" (the sea, the sun, the air), but this very "polytheistic" response to nature "swallows up the individual life." And finally Camus' "philosophical intention is too obvious in all his imaginative writing." Hence his fictions seem contrived. His real importance is that he recalls for us "an awareness of the human condition"; as a dramatist and imaginative writer he is not of the first importance.

The Aesthetics Of Camus

In fact comparatively little has been written concerning Camus as an imaginative writer. Most of the criticism so far surveyed has been directed to an analysis of Camus as a philosopher, moralist, and conscience. The reader will find, however, in Sartre's essay some remarks on Camus' style, his use of language, his novelistic inventions, especially in his peculiarly effective use of the simple sentence, the verb, and tense. "Each sentence," Sartre notes of *The Stranger*, "is a present instant-sharp, distinct, and self-contained. . . The world is destroyed and reborn from sentence to sentence." Such sentences recreate exactly the absurd world of Meursault, for whom only the present instant exists. Robert Champigny, in his essay "Ethics and Aesthetics in *The Stranger*," shows how the literary structure and techniques of that novel are related to the ethical points being made by Camus, demonstrating that the form and content resonate with one another. "As we read it," he says, "or perhaps reread it, the monologue of Meursault appears as the equivalent of a novel called *The Stranger*." S. Beynon John investigates the **imagery** in the work of Camus in an essay called "Image and Symbol in the Work of Camus." He shows that the image of the sun and sea are so persistent in the work of Camus that they acquire symbolic force. The sea becomes identified with free existence. It is the source of life and in man acquires freedom. He notes, for example, the importance of the sea in *The State of Siege*, in *The Plague*, and in *The Stranger*, where it always symbolizes more or less the same thing. He relates these persistent images which take on symbolic density to Camus' belief that every writer attempts to recreate the two or three images that come to him with obsessive force from his childhood. Other analyses of Camus' style may be found in the work of Bree and Thody. In his essay "Notes on *The Plague*," Gaetan Picon analyzes the various levels on which the novel is meaningful: the realistic, the allegorical, the philosophical. The difficulties Camus has in molding these levels together are noted. He shows how the very identification of the plague with Death and the hostility of the universe to man forces Camus into a position where the characters in his novel cannot act with a **realism** which the reader can accept.

Exile And The Kingdom

This work represents for Picon a movement away from abstraction. Here Camus seems more interested in men and women for their own sakes. Abstraction is beginning to recede into the background. In it for the first time there is the notion that man has a "kingdom" in which he can be happy, not as a condition for which one must strive, but as a real thing that is here. In this work "the moralist who isolates and dissects is succeeded by the poet who puts together and restores the one complex throb of life."

Camus As Playwright

Major portions of Bree and Thody's books are given over to an analysis of Camus' plays. However, both these critics are concerned primarily, though not exclusively, with the thought of Camus. Henry Popkin, in his essay "Camus as Dramatist," is concerned with the dramatic techniques of Camus: that is, primarily with Camus' theater. His dramas, "simple in plot, direct in argument, oratorically eloquent," are "like few other modern plays. They are closest to Gide and to the Sartre of the early plays (*No Exit* and *The Flies*)" "before Sartre mastered the deceptions . . . of the stage." Camus dramatizes-unlike Cocteau, Giraudoux, and Sartre-forthrightly "with tricks, no sneers, no 'modernization.'" Camus' classical restraint never allows him any lushness for "the sake of theatricality." Whatever is there is the absolute minimum that needs to be there. The plays are, in keeping with this, constructed on simple formulas. The language is "lofty and pure." It is, however, this very desire on the part of Camus to use elevated language which is his defect as a playwright. What he avoided in his novels-becoming a "pamphleteer" and propagandist for his philosophy-he did not avoid in his plays, with the exception of *Caligula*. If any play of Camus continues to hold the stage it will be *Caligula*. Eric Bently in his book The Playwright as Thinker devotes considerable attention to Camus.

Final Estimate

It is, of course, impossible to fix anyone's stature or importance absolutely. Reputations rise and fall. Time passes and certain habitual attitudes grow up concerning men of the past. In spite of his age when he died, he created a reputation in his own time as solid and important as those that usually come to men only after long lives or even after their deaths. In his own time he was admitted into the temple of French classics. Whether this reputation will endure we cannot know. It is, therefore, perhaps fitting that we close this survey of Camus' reputation with a quotation from Sartre who, in "Tribute to Albert Camus" printed shortly after Camus' death, came forward to praise his old friend with whom he had quarreled. "Insofar as Camus' humanism contains a human attitude towards the death that was to take him by surprise, insofar as his proud and pure quest for happiness implied and called for the inhuman necessity of dying, we shall recognize in that work and in the life that is inseparable from it the pure and victorious attempt of one man to snatch every instant of his existence from his future death."

THE PLAYS

It is the general opinion of critics that Camus' greatest strength as a writer is to be found in his novels, stories, and essays, not in his plays. However, this is a relative, not an absolute judgment. The plays are well worth knowing for two reasons: they are good in themselves, and they are indispensable to a full understanding of Camus' complexity as a creative writer involved in the major problems of modern times. All of the plays without exception are dramatizations of Camus' central concerns: the dangers of nihilism, totalitarianism, the possibility of justice, and true and false rebels. *Caligula* deals with the problem of nihilism as it leads to absolute excess and tyranny. *The State of Siege* deals with the same situation as does *The Plague*, only here the plague is limited to a definite identification with totalitarianism. *The Just Assassins* deals with the problem of true rebellion and false revolt and confronts the notions of limits and absolutes. *The Misunderstanding* dramatizes the little newspaper account (of the return of the wealthy Czech to his home only to be murdered by his mother and sister) which constituted all of Meursault's reading material in prison in *The Stranger*. This play deals more generally with the antagonism between man and existence which Camus finds at the heart of life. In the plays, Camus establishes his theses in simpler terms, and because of this the plays provide an easier approach to his thought. But this very simplicity of presentation has the effect of blurring the complicated edges of Camus' thought. In the plays he tends to present his case in more extreme form than in the novels and essays.

Comment

Caligula is perhaps the most powerful of all Camus' original plays. The language is lean, hard, and supple. The character of Caligula achieves tragic stature because of his excess. Like Prometheus, Oedipus, Antigone, and Creon his commitment to his point of view is absolute. All Greek tragic figures suffer because of a lack of moderation. Caligula takes on these same dimensions because he cannot live with half measures. The very effect of a tragic figure is to demonstrate to the audience the necessity of moderation: "nothing in excess." But in a paradoxical sense it is the function of tragic heroes to go to excess in order to demonstrate limits. Cherea represents, like the Greek chorus, the ordinary human values: he merely wishes to be happy. But Camus shows in this play that no single person can be happy, or free, which for Camus is the same thing, at the expense of the happiness of others. He shows how nihilism can lead to tyranny. Cherea has gone beyond nihilism and constructed an ethic out of his belief that life, merely in its own terms, can be meaningful. But the fact that Cherea and Scipio use Caligula's method (murder) to bring about the end of his tyranny demonstrates that, as he dies, he speaks the truth. He is still alive. The reader recalls the final passages of *The Plague* in which Dr. Rieux says that the people rejoicing outside are living in illusion. The plague is still alive. The rats will appear in the streets of the "happy city" again. It is this identification of Caligula with the universal condition of mankind which gives it a more than local meaning. For Caligula is finally evil not because he has killed and murdered but because he has joined with the forces of death against life.

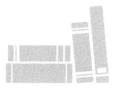

THE PLAYS

THE STATE OF SIEGE

· ·

The State of Siege is Camus' fourth play. It was presented first in October of 1948 in Jean-Louis Barroult's production at the Theatre Marigny. The subject of the play is the same as that of *The Plague*, but the realization is completely different. Here the plague is manifest in the form of a human dictator. In the first production he was played by an actor in Nazi uniform. But Camus would have preferred the actor to wear the costume of a civil servant. The scene is laid in Spain, in the city of Cadiz. When questioned about this, Camus answered that it was to widen his identification of the enemy, for it is not only the ideologies of the Left but also of the Right he is attacking-all forms of dictatorship. Camus called it a morality play, an allegorical treatment of a subject known to the whole audience in advance. He says that he concentrated on what he believed was the "only living religion in the century of tyrants and slaves"-liberty. He wanted to cut out psychological speculation for the purpose of giving room to the "loud shouts that today enslave or liberate masses of men." He points out that the play has never been produced in Russia or in Spain and that he was attempting to enlighten his audience's judgment, not influence it. It is perhaps Camus' most experimental play. In it he attempts to mingle "all the different forms of dramatic expression." In it we find the lyrical monologue, pantomime, traditional dialogue, farce, and a chorus.

THE PLAYS

THE MISUNDERSTANDING

Camus wrote *The Misunderstanding* in 1943 in occupied France. It is another of Camus' "modern tragedies." A son who "expects to be recognized without having to declare his name and who is killed by his mother and his sister as the result of the misunderstanding"-such is the subject of the play. Camus constructed a language for the play that would be appropriate to a "modern tragedy." He wished to give "aloofness to the characters and ambiguity to the dialogue." He wished in fact to achieve a double focus, one which would show, at one and the same time, a contemporary situation under the aspect of an unchanging human condition. One critic (Thody: see Bibliography) believes that he has succeeded in creating a true tragedy. Such was not the opinion of the audience, nor has it been the opinion of most critics, who feel that the characters do not take on sufficient depth and merely serve to illustrate the problem Camus has set himself to work out. There is also the fact that the language does not work; it is too artificial in the wrong way. But the play is still interesting as it shows Camus' constant preoccupation with the problem of death and the human condition.

THE PLAYS

THE JUST ASSASSINS

. . . .

For the subject of *The Just Assassins* Camus went, for the first time, to history. The setting is Moscow in 1905. The cast is small, the stage sets are harsh, stingy with properties. Appropriately the language is hard and peeled of all ornament. The event itself has a clean and classic outline. The Russian terrorist and revolutionary Boris Savinkov had provided its outline in his book *Recollections of a Terrorist*. The combat organization of the Socialist party had decided to assassinate the Grand Duke Sergei Alexandrovich. Two men, Kaliayev and Alexandrovich, are detailed to hurl a bomb into the carriage of the Grand Duke. At the appointed time, Kaliayev does not throw the bomb. The Grand Duke has two small children with him. The children are innocent. Can they, in order to carry out their plans for a just society, kill the innocent? One argues "yes," for the future happiness of mankind. But, says Kaliayev, how can he add to the present suffering and pain of the world he knows for a future he does not know? This argument carries the day. The innocent must be spared. This problem-how far the rebel can be allowed to inflict pain and punishment in order to assure his own integrity and the happiness of mankind-is central to Camus. He offers, throughout his many books and plays, a great number

THE STRANGER AND OTHER WORKS

of possible answers, ranging from Tarrou's total abnegation of violence through the position of Cherea and Scipio, who react violently only when pushed into a corner, to that of Kaliayev and his group, who permit violence even when they themselves are not actually threatened, to the opposite position of such persons as Othon, who joins, passively, the establishment, and Nada, who actively works with the enemy. It is difficult to say whether Camus advocates any of the rebellious positions. As he says, his books and plays were written not to influence judgment but to illuminate it.

THE PLAYS

Although Camus wrote only four original plays, he adapted a considerable number of others, from Greek, Italian, Spanish, and English. As well as devoting much of his energy to this task of making the plays of other times and cultures available to his audience, he also adapted many novels, reconstructing them as plays. The two most important of these are *Requiem for a Nun* and *The Possessed*. The first of these is adapted from William Faulkner's novel of the same name, the second from Dostoevsky's novel *The Possessed*. The Faulkner novel is a sequel to *Sanctuary*. In that novel, Temple Drake, a judge's daughter, had been raped and put in a house of prostitution in Memphis. Later she marries. In *Requiem for a Nun*, a woman, Nancy, is on trial for the murder of Temple's child. Eventually Nancy is condemned to death, but it is brought out in the trial that Temple and Nancy had been in the brothel together, and the child's death is seen as a sacrifice for Temple's guilt. Nancy is Camus' heroine. She represents common ordinary humanity crushed and pressed by the system which is allied with Death.

This same pattern reappears in *The Possessed*. A group of young men "possessed" by revolution set out to make life meaningful by acts of violence. They end by killing Shatov, an innocent young man. Stavrogin, the main character, commits suicide. Since Stavrogin, like Caligula, cannot see beyond nihilism, the murder and the suicide are inevitable. When one sinks into nihilism, one is blind to the ordinary human values. All one feels, like Caligula and de Sade, is "scorn." Scorn, becoming habitual, ends in hate; and the nihilists hate love, friendship, compassion, humor, the joy of life, and the common aspirations of ordinary men. Up to the time of this play, Camus had concentrated more on showing life from the position of the nihilist. The general impression one gets from his work is seriousness, weight; if there is humor (and there is), or compassion (and there is), it tends to be given from a distance, from a long perspective. There are indications that Camus was beginning to move these values into the center of his stage. At the end of his life he was working on a novel *The First Man*, where there elements perhaps would have played a greater part. He was also devoting much of his time to a play about Don Juan. It is hard to see how he could treat this subject without humor and compassion. In fact his last published novel, *The Fall*, and many of the stories in *Exile and the Kingdom* already show these characteristics.

THE PLAYS

Question: Is Camus a great dramatist, say, of the order of Ibsen or Shaw?

Answer: The Answer to this question must be no. Although Ibsen and Shaw, like Camus, wrote directly from a platform of social and, often, political criticism, their dramatic energy was greater, their ability to invent living characters greater, their objectification of the material they worked with greater than anything Camus achieved. Camus, like both of these men and like Shakespeare and the Greek playwrights (Sophocles and Aeschylus especially) whom he so much admired, knew the theater intimately, as actor and director as well as writer. Certainly this knowledge aided immeasurably in making Camus' plays actable. He knows how to stage an exit, an entrance, build to a **climax**, and move through action and dialogue from one scene to another. But in the last analysis Camus' theater is weakened by his very strength: he is a thesis playwright. Essentially a moralist, he was never completely concerned with characters for their own sakes, as the great playwright always is, and only secondarily with what they represent. This is the same weakness that can be charged against the novels. No character of Camus, with the possible exception of the demoniac Caligula, and the curiously charming Meursault, ever escapes from the author's grasp. Vital and dynamic as many are, their dynamism and vitality are, perhaps, really the result of Camus' energy of thought rather than his energy of creativity. The theater of ideas has never been popular except with a certain limited portion of the population. Camus' popularity as a playwright is today pretty well confined to productions by little theaters and college groups.

Question: Much of Camus' philosophy is concerned with the notion of the absurd. Is Camus' theater properly placed with the so-called "theater of the absurd," the theater of such playwrights as Brecht, Ionesco, Genet, and Albee?

Answer: No, The "theater of the absurd" is generated by the commitment to the belief that life is, when viewed rationally, dead and so systematically abstracted as to be incomprehensible. The only logical way to understand existence is "irrationally." This accounts for the heavy use of symbolic modes in the theater of the absurd: the dislocations of time and space, the elimination of traditional connectives, the use of tableaux, puppets, machines, and the like. Shakespeare said "We are such stuff as dreams are made of"; the playwrights of the absurd, having the benefit of Freud, say "We are such stuff as nightmares are made of." What they seek to present is not the rationale of the intellect, but the reason of the psyche. They follow Pascal's dictum that "the heart has reasons which the mind knows nothing of." When they are successful, as in Genet in such a play as *The Blacks*, the impact on the audience is incredible. But few indeed are those blessed with the ability to delve at any depth in the unconscious mind. Camus on the other hand, in spite of his sense of the absurd, is committed to rationality. This is shown by the total intellectuality of his work; his sentences, in their rhythm and shape, are patterned on Chateaubriand and the great tradition of the eighteenth century, the "Age of Reason." His sense of plot is drawn from the Greeks and from the French classicists, Racine and Corneille. His plays attempt, as do his essays and novels, to bring the force of intellect, informed, cleansed, and strengthened by conscience, to bear on contemporary problems. In a true sense, he was constantly attempting to bring into the clearing of rationality more and more territory, territory which was constantly threatening to slip back into the jungles of chaos and mindlessness. In this he joined the Greeks. What is the *Odyssey* after all but an attempt to clear out of chaos a territory of reason where the human community could exist in mutual justice?

Question: What basic pattern do all of Camus' plays follow?

Answer: The basic pattern of all Camus' plays is this: the normal human community, "the order of ordinary values," is dislocated by some force or other, which may be identified as the plague, or death; some system comes into the ascendancy which, because it is excessive, ends in the denial of order, in a sense it is a systematic disorder (*The State of Siege*, *The Plague*). Perversions of the notions of what is good and what is evil follow; life becomes meaningless; men's reason for being is taken from them (*Caligula*). Then there is a reaction. Some rebel; this rebellion, started in isolation, leads to solidarity, and the "plague" is overthrown; the natural order reasserts its sovereignty. But this primacy of the natural order is temporary. One must constantly be on guard. The rock of Sisyphus rolls down the mountain again; Caligula screams "I'm still alive"; the rats will reappear in the "happy city."

Question: Is the philosophy of Camus, as evidenced in his plays, basically pessimistic or optimistic?

Answer: It would be possible, by selecting certain features of Camus' work, to present a case on either side. But the truth is that Camus can only be called a realist. A realist is one who does not hide his head in the sand. Camus sees in man a recurrent and forceful attraction to what can only be called evil. When, for one reason or another, enough men, consciously or unconsciously, side with death in any form, the ordinary human community is in danger. But he also believes that some members of the ordinary human community will fight to reassert the "common values." Existence then is a seesaw in which some strive for the balance where life can be happy. There are others who always wish their side of the bar to be up or down. Balance is moderation. Justice is the harmony in which the integrity of all is preserved. But watchfulness is needed. Education inculcates watchfulness. On the one hand we have sentimentalists, who cannot believe that anyone is really committed to death and evil. "I like old Joe," as someone said of the man (Stalin) who had systematically destroyed millions of people. "There'll be peace in our time," as someone said after honoring Hitler's agreement. This pollyanna belief in the essential goodness of man is merely ignorance of the human potential for evil. The cynic on the other hand is an inverted sentimentalist. He believes that all men are corrupted and given to evil. He is willing to believe the bad much more readily than the good. Everyone can be bought; there is an angle to everything one does. Camus, as do most mature and reasonable men, stands in the middle. If standing in the middle can be called the attitude of the optimist, then Camus is an optimist. The liberal humanist today is often weakened by his sentimental belief that all men are good and that if they do evil it is not they who are at fault but circumstances. Camus refocuses the reality of the true liberal humanist position: men are capable of all things-hence let us work to make sure that they will seek to do only some.

BIBLIOGRAPHY

For the most part only those books and articles are listed which are available in English.

WORKS BY CAMUS IN BOOK FORM

Betwixt and Between, Algiers: Charlot, 1936.

Nuptials, Algiers: Charlot, 1938.

The Stranger, Paris: Gallimard, 1942.

The Myth of Sisyphus, Paris: Gallimard, 1942.

Letters to a German Friend, Paris: Gallimard, 1945.

The Misunderstanding and *Caligula*, Paris: Gallimard, 1945.

The Plague, Paris: Gallimard, 1948.

The Just Assassins, Paris: Gallimard, 1950.

The Rebel, Paris: Gallimard, 1951.

Summer, Paris: Gallimard, 1954.

The Fall, Paris: Gallimard, 1956.

Exile and the Kingdom, Paris: Gallimard, 1957.

BOOKS ON CAMUS

Bree, Germaine. *Camus*. New Brunswick: Rutgers University Press, 1959;
    rev. ed., 1961.

Bree, Germaine, ed. *Camus: A Collection of Critical Essays*, Englewood Cliffs:
    Prentice-Hall, 1962. Paperback.

Cruickshank, John. *Albert Camus*, London: Oxford University Press, 1959;
    New York: Galaxy Books, 1960. Paperback.

Hanna, Thomas. *The Thought and Art of Albert Camus*, Chicago: Henry Regnery,
    1958.

Maquet, Albert. *Albert Camus: The Invincible Summer*, Herma Brissault, tr.,
    New York: George Braziller, 1958.

Thody, Philip. *Albert Camus: A Study of His Work*, New York: Macmillan, 1957.

ARTICLES ON CAMUS

(In the order of their publication)

Ayer, A. J. "Novelist-Philosophers," *Horizon*, March, 1946.

Heppenstall, Rayner. "Albert Camus and the Romantic Protest," in *Penguin New Writing*, No. 34, 1948, 104-116.

Bree, Germaine. "Introduction to Albert Camus," *French Studies*, 1 (1950), 27-37.

John, S. B. "Image and Symbol in Albert Camus," *French Studies* (January, 1955), 42-53.

Wollheim, Richard. "The Political Philosophy of Existentialism," *Cambridge Journal* (October, 1953), 3-19.

Stockwell, H. R. "Albert Camus," *Cambridge Journal* (August, 1954), 690-704.

Roth, Leon. "Albert Camus," *Philosophy* (October, 1955), 291-303.

Cruickshank, J. "Camus' Technique in *L'Etranger*," *French Studies* (Autumn, 1955).

BOOKS WITH SECTIONS ON CAMUS

Collins, James D. *The Existentials: A Critical Study*, Chicago: Henry Regnery, 1952.

Copleston, F. C. *Existentialism and Modern Man*, London: Blackfriars Publications, 1953.

Curtis, Anthony. *New Developments in the French Theatre*, London: The Curtain Press, 1948.

Gassner, John. *Masters of the Drama*, New York: Dover Publications, 1954.

Kaufmann, Walter A. *Existentialism from Dostoevsky to Sartre*, New York: Meridian Books, 1956. Paperback.

Lerner, Max. *Actions and Passions: Notes on the Multiple Revolutions of Our Time*, New York: Simon and Schuster, 1949.

Sartre, Jean-Paul. *Literary and Philosophical Essays*, Annette Michelson, tr., New York: Criterion Books, 1955.

Lightning Source UK Ltd.
Milton Keynes UK
UKHW021604260721
387787UK00011B/2438